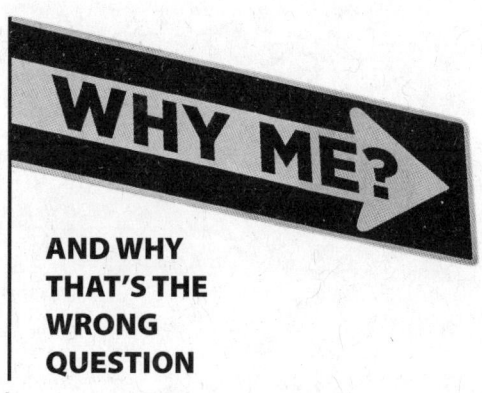

**AND WHY
THAT'S THE
WRONG
QUESTION**

AND WHY THAT'S THE WRONG QUESTION

A Godly View of Suffering

Jim Davis

WHY ME? (AND WHY THAT'S THE WRONG QUESTION)
A Godly View of Suffering

ISBN 978-0-89112-455-9 | LCCN 2013041824

Copyright © 2014 by Jim Davis. Printed in the United States of America. ALL RIGHTS RESERVED. No part of this publication may be reproduced, stored in a retrieval system, or transmitted in any form by any means—electronic, mechanical, photocopying, recording, or otherwise—without prior written consent.

Scripture quotations, unless otherwise noted, are from The Holy Bible, New International Version®, NIV®. Copyright ©1973, 1978, 1984, 2011 by Biblica, Inc.™ Used by permission. All rights reserved worldwide.

Scripture quotations noted ESV are from The Holy Bible, English Standard Version® (ESV®), copyright © 2001 by Crossway, a publishing ministry of Good News Publishers. All rights reserved.

Scriptures noted NKJV are taken from the New King James Version. Copyright © 1982 by Thomas Nelson, Inc. Used by permission. All rights reserved.

Scripture quotations noted *The Message* are taken from *The Message*. Copyright © 1993, 1994, 1995, 1996, 2000, 2001, 2002. Used by permission of NavPress Publishing Group.

Scripture quotations noted NLT are taken from the New Living Translation, copyright ©1996, 2004. Used by permission of Tyndale House Publishers, Inc., Carol Stream, Illinois 60188. All rights reserved.

Scripture quotations marked HCSB are taken from the Holman Christian Standard Bible®, Copyright © 1999, 2000, 2002, 2009 by Holman Bible Publishers. Used by permission. Holman Christian Standard Bible®, Holman CSB®, and HCSB® are federally registered trademarks of Holman Bible Publishers.

Scripture quotations marked PHILLIPS are taken from The New Testament in Modern English, copyright © 1958, 1960, 1972 J.B. Phillips. Used by permission of Macmillan Publishing Company.

Scripture quotations noted NASB are taken from the New American Standard Bible®, Copyright © 1960, 1963, 1968, 1971, 1972, 1973, 1975, 1977, 1995 The Lockman Foundation. Used by permission.

Scripture quotations marked NLV are taken from the NEW LIFE Version, © Christian Literature International.

Scripture quotations marked NCV are taken from the New Century Version®. Copyright © 1987, 1988, 1991 by Thomas Nelson, Inc. Used by permission. All rights reserved.

Scripture quotations noted KJV are taken from the King James Version of the Bible.

Scripture quotations marked ASV are taken from the American Standard Version of the Bible.

Published in association with the Seymour Agency, 475 Miner Street Road, Canton, NY 13617.

LIBRARY OF CONGRESS CATALOGING-IN-PUBLICATION DATA
Davis, Jim, 1968-
  Why me? (and why that's the wrong question) : a godly view of suffering / Jim Davis.
     pages cm
  Includes bibliographical references and index.
  ISBN 978-0-89112-455-9 (alk. paper)
  1. Suffering--Religious aspects--Christianity. 2. Providence and government of God--Christianity. I. Title.
  BT732.7.D375 2014
  231'.8--dc23

2013041824

Cover design by Thinkpen Design, LLC | Interior text design by Sandy Armstrong, Strong Design
For information, contact: Abilene Christian University Press
1626 Campus Court, Abilene, Texas 79601
1-877-816-4455 | www.leafwoodpublishers.com

14 15 16 17 18 19 / 7 6 5 4 3 2 1

To Sonya and Tully.

*To Crickett and Sue,
in thanks for their encouragement and friendship.*

*To Blue Dragon and the Monday-night men's group,
and all other friends and family who offered feedback.*

*To Mike, April, and Trent Reed; Mike and Pam Worley;
Clay and Melanie Brewer; and others who shared their stories
so that God may be glorified.*

*To all those who are suffering, or who will suffer,
and who question the goodness of God.
You are not alone and you are deeply loved.*

CONTENTS

Introduction 9

Part One
Why We Ask Questions

1. The Search for Answers 17
2. The Root of Our Questions 29
   Mike and Mike (1) 39

Part Two
The Wrong Questions

3. Why Me?
   (Because Everyone Hurts) 47
4. Why Do Bad Things Happen to Good People? Part One
   (What Good People?) 59
5. Why Do Bad Things Happen to Good People? Part Two
   (Is It Really a "Bad" Thing?) 69
   The Voyage of Life 83
6. Does God Care?
   (Of Course He Does) 85
7. Why Doesn't God Do Something?
   (He Has, He Is, and He Will) 97
8. Where's My Miracle?
   (It May Be Better Than You Dared Hope) 111
   Mike and Mike (2) 127

Part Three
The Right Questions

9. How Can This Trial Draw Me Closer to God? 139
10. How Can This Trial Help Me Become More Like Jesus? 151
11. How Can I Glorify God in My Suffering? 165
    My Journey to Joy (A Testimony by Marie Hillstrom) 179

12. How Can This Trial Help Me Minister to Others
    Who Are Suffering?..183
13. Can I Really Rejoice in My Trials?..193
    Mike and Mike (3)..207
    Conclusion..213

Study Questions 219
Bibliography 237

INTRODUCTION

1
Why me, you ask?

Well, why not you? Why not me? Everyone suffers at some point, in some way, in this world. The death rate is 100 percent. Cancer plays no favorites, and automobile accidents happen to murderers and pastors alike. Every day loved ones die, businesses fail, homes are flattened, and relationships are challenged. It's a fallen world, and no one gets through it without some knocks. I'll admit that some people seem to have more than their share, but everybody hurts in some way, sometime.

Why do bad things happen to good people, you ask?

Well, who are we to decide who is good and who is bad? Who are we to decide who deserves to suffer and who does not? We can't even always tell the good news from the bad.

Why doesn't God do something, you ask?

Who says he hasn't done something already, when he came to live with us and died for our sins? Or who says that he isn't doing something at the moment you question him, when he may be acting in unseen ways to give you peace, or to send friends to love you in your pain? It may not always be the way we wish he would act, but God is at work.

I'm not tossing your questions aside. Your questions are valid and understandable (although, as we'll see, they may rest on a shaky foundation). When we have problems, we *all* want to know why. Desperately so. When a crazed gunman enters an elementary school or a movie theater,

WHY ME? (And Why That's the Wrong Question)

when the doctor about to share test results can't look us in the eye, when our employer moves in a "new direction," when a spouse breaks vows, or when we lay fresh flowers on top of a mound of upturned earth, we want to know why. We don't understand why God lets bad things happen, or why they happen to us or the people we love in particular. We think life should be better than it is, and it's maddening that a God who is loving and all-powerful won't make it so. Something doesn't fit, and we have lots of different ways of asking why not. Especially when the hurt is fresh.

These questions—the "why me" questions—are universal. I ask them, too, and as a Sunday-school teacher for nearly twenty years, I have heard others ask them time and time again. In classes I have taught, there have been countless trials, such as job loss, illness, marital problems, fire, service overseas, and a funeral with a tiny white casket. Every week we hear about a new batch of pain, and every week we ask, "Why?"

As I heard these questions over and over, I grew tired of having nothing but a shrug to offer. That set me on a journey to see what smart people have concluded about the "why me" questions and what the Bible says about them. I went looking for answers, but they weren't there, and instead I learned that I should focus on a completely different set of questions.

What I learned from the experts and philosophers during my search was not much of any practical help. First of all, even if I knew *why* pain exists, it would still hurt. And second, there was absolutely no consensus on the matter. While most of the many books that try to explain suffering are written with the best of intentions, there are as many different ideas about why the world includes pain as there are people who write about it. There are a lot of guesses, but no one seems to *know*. Although hurting people throughout Scripture ask why certain things happen, God does not answer the "why me" questions, no matter how many times they ask.

And while we wait on an answer that isn't coming, we rarely pause to wonder if our "why me" questions make sense in light of the truths of

Scripture. What right do we have to expect to avoid the bad stuff, when God never promised that this life would be free of sorrow, and he is in fact quite clear that the opposite is true? How can we persist in a view that God doesn't care about our suffering when Scripture shows that nothing can be further from the truth?

Another problem with the "why me" questions is what they do to our relationship with God. And here I don't mean raising the questions while the cut is still bleeding, which we all do, and which may even be an important part of the grieving process. I mean the damage that is done when we dwell on those questions for a prolonged period. It's hard to stay close to God when our hands are on our hips and we demand that God explain himself. As I thought and studied about trials, I saw that if a person was growing more and more bitter as a result of suffering, that person usually was obsessing over the "why me" questions long after the trial was over.

But those are not the only questions we can ask about suffering. In my observations, I saw that some people move on eventually and start thinking about other things. The people who came through the trial on their feet, who grew stronger as a result of the storm, were the ones who began to ask questions that focused on God and not on themselves: *How can God use this trial for good? How can God be glorified? How can this trial help me minister to others?*

This book is about the two kinds of questions people ask about suffering. In Part One, we will examine our search for answers about suffering and why we ask questions in the first place. Then, in Part Two, we will dissect the "why me" questions that everyone seems to ask at first. These I call the "wrong" questions because they are not answered in the Bible or anywhere else, they do not lead to healing, and they usually reveal a misunderstanding about our fallen world and our loving God. Finally, in Part Three, we will study the God-centered questions I call the "right" questions. We can find answers to those. The Father explains clearly how he can use trials for good, how he can be glorified, and how he can help us become more like his Son as a result of our pain. The right questions lead to healing and strengthen our faith.

It matters what you ask about suffering. Sooner or later, we are all going to go through it. When that day comes for you, you can get stuck in the wrong questions, pull away from God, watch your faith wither away, and spend the rest of your days complaining that life is unfair. Or, you can move on to the right questions and look for the good that can arise out of suffering—acknowledging God's sovereignty, remembering his love, and strengthening your faith.

The questions you ask will, I believe, have a lot to do with whether your trials defeat you or make you stronger. My hope is that this study will help you see that the wrong questions lead down a dangerous path, so that when the storm comes for you, you will be able eventually to move on to questions that lead to healing and fellowship.

We have a choice, you see. Not whether we will know pain, but how we will respond. We can say, "This hurts; I don't understand, so I will be mad at God until the day I die." Or, we can say, "This hurts; I don't understand, but I will love God and trust him until the day I die."

It hurts when life isn't perfect, but it really shouldn't be surprising. Now, *before* the trial, is the time to decide what questions to ask. God has made it pretty clear that he isn't going to answer the wrong questions. The right questions, though . . . he has a lot say about those.

When we stop asking "why me" and start asking "what can God do with this," it changes *everything*.

Cast your cares on the LORD and he will sustain you; he will never let the righteous be shaken. (Ps. 55:22)

2

If you have recently suffered a tragedy, I want you to know up front that this book is not meant to be a guide to the grieving process. It is instead a study of what the Bible reveals about suffering and our effort to understand it. The book asks whether our usual questions make sense in the light of Scripture and whether there are more productive questions we could be asking. While I hope there is comfort in these pages (the book is about God's Word, and God is our comforter), I did not write them specifically for the mourning, but for anyone, in any season, who is concerned about the question of God's goodness in the face of suffering.

If you want to explore what the Bible says about the questions we ask, that's what you will find here. If you want to lay down a foundation of faith now, before (or after) the storm hits, which will help you turn *to* God during a trial and not away from him, then let's dig in.

PART ONE

Why We Ask Questions

THE SEARCH FOR ANSWERS

> Everyone asks *why me* at some point, including many faithful people in the Bible (like Job). It's human nature to wonder why bad things happen. Thus far, though, God has not answered those questions.

1

The plaque hung just outside the principal's office at my high school, not far from my locker. "In memory of," it said, listing the names of three teenagers who died in a car accident on their way to the beach in 1971, the summer before their senior year. I do not remember the accident at all—I was very young at the time—and have only the vaguest memories of my uncle Joe, one of the young men who perished.

There is a new school now, and I wonder if the plaque made the move.

By the time I was seventeen, the age that Joe and his friends were when they died, hardly anyone noticed the memorial as we fetched books between classes. But at the time, how that crash must have rocked our small town. The death of one teenager goes against the natural order of things and is bad enough. Three at one time seems more than a small town could bear.

I wonder what the three boys would have been like now, if they or the truck they met had not gone through DeFuniak Springs. Would they be husbands and fathers? Grandfathers? Community leaders? What would their jobs be? How much was our town missing as a result of one violent moment? And how many times did those three families wonder, "Why?"

> *Will you never look away from me, or let me alone even for an instant?... Why have you made me your target? (Job 7:19–20)*

2

You're not the first person to ask, "Why me?" You are not the first to ask any of the questions you are pondering from a doctor's waiting room, or hunched over a checkbook with more red than black. You are in pretty good company, as a matter of fact.

The woman down the street whose husband just moved out, and who is wondering what kind of job she can get that will cover more than day care? She's asked it.

The guy at work arranging for family leave to spend more time in the pediatric oncology ward? I bet it's crossed his mind.

That couple who stopped coming to Sunday school? You won't find out the reason for a while, but they're asking it, too.

There are people everywhere, all around you, who have something going on and wonder why it's happening to them. It may not be for the same reason as you, and you may think that your reason for asking is more valid, but they're all asking the same question: "Why me?"

It's a universal question. You'll even find it asked in the Bible. Take Job, for instance. Every study of suffering gets to Job sooner or later, and for good reason. The entire book is about that most basic of human questions and how God doesn't answer it.

In the land of Uz long, long ago, when wealth and prosperity were measured in children and livestock, Job had it all: seven sons, three daughters, servants, thousands of sheep, oxen, camels, and donkeys. And he was godly to boot, a respected sage in the community, "the greatest man among all the people of the East" (Job 1:3b). Then a series of messengers came to Job, one after the other, to tell him he had lost it all.

"*Your oxen and donkeys? Gone. Lost to a Sabean raiding party.*"

"*Your sheep? Gone. Fire from heaven.*"

"*Your camels? Gone. Lost in a Chaldean attack.*"

In the blink of an eye, Job went from the richest man in the East to one of the poorest. And before anyone could say, *But that's just stuff; at least you still have what's important,* a fourth messenger arrived: "Your sons and daughters were feasting and drinking wine at the oldest brother's house, when suddenly a mighty wind swept in from the desert and struck the four corners of the house. It collapsed on them and they are dead, and I am the only one who has escaped to tell you!" (Job 1:18b–19). (As it turns out, Satan was the cause of Job's troubles, having received permission from God to torment Job, a fact which makes my head hurt. That information was never given to Job, as far as we know.)

Suffering is not a contest,[1] but even the worst of what we go through hardly measures up to Job's very bad day. Still, his initial response was not a question, but praise: "Naked I came from my mother's womb, and naked I will depart. The LORD gave and the LORD has taken away; may the name of the LORD be praised" (Job 1:21).

Of course, that wasn't the last word. Job's physical health was attacked next when he was afflicted with "painful sores from the soles of his feet to the crown of his head" (Job 2:7). I don't know if the sores were the last straw or if Job just had time to be human, but his response changed: "Why did I not perish at birth, and die as I came from the womb?" (Job 3:11).

And then, looking up to heaven, Job asks the same question so many of us have asked: "Why have you made me your target?" (Job 7:20b).

See? You're not alone.

> *Why have you brought this trouble on your servant? What have I done to displease you? (Num. 11:11)*

3

There is a name for it, this search for answers. That alone ought to tell you that you aren't weird for asking the questions you are asking. It's called *theodicy*, and it is, according to *Merriam-Webster's Collegiate Dictionary*, the "defense of God's goodness and omnipotence in view of the existence of evil."

For as long as there has been suffering—since the fall of Adam and Eve, that is—people have been trying to figure out how different things they believe to be true can be true at the same time. God is good, he tells us. Perfect, in fact. And he is all-powerful. There is nothing that God cannot do.

But if that is so, people ask, then why is there evil and suffering in the world? Why would a perfectly good, all-powerful God allow pain and trials to enter the world at all? This so-called inconsistency has led some philosophers to conclude that God must not exist. The ancient Greek philosopher Epicurus was the first (some think) to put it something like this:

- If there is a God who is perfectly good, he would stop evil if he could.
- If God is also all-powerful, he *could* stop evil.
- Evil certainly does exist.
- Therefore, a perfectly good, all-powerful God must not exist.

Theodicy is the response to such arguments, and a *lot* of writers have tried to prove Epicurus wrong.

C. S. Lewis wrote that evil exists because God gives us free will, and we are naughty to our core. If God removed evil—if he took away all the consequences of our evil thoughts and deeds—free will wouldn't mean anything. How could we have free will to cause pain, if God miraculously stopped all our bullets?[2] (This explanation makes quite a bit of sense to me, but I may be predisposed to agree with someone I admire as much as I do Lewis. However, while I believe that Lewis's answer is logical and *consistent* with Scripture, it is not necessarily *mandated* by Scripture. It is a question—as Job learns—that God simply does not answer.)

German philosopher Gottfried Leibniz (who coined the word *theodicy*) put forth the "best of all possible worlds" defense way back in 1710. He believed good and evil *must* exist together in some form. God could create any kind of world he wanted to, and because he is inherently good, we can have confidence that this world is the very best combination of good and evil of all the combinations possible.[3] That assumes, of course, that it was impossible for God to create a world where evil would never arise, when the Bible says plainly that "with God all things are possible" (Matt. 19:26).

Some have concluded that all evil and hardship is because of Satan, and while I believe Satan is real, is he really responsible for every pink slip and stubbed toe? Others believe that suffering is just an illusion, which is silly. Pain is all too obviously real. And, as discussed above, some have simply concluded that there must not be a god, which gives up any hope we have of making sense of all this.

The most famous book on the subject may be the one by Rabbi Harold Kushner, *When Bad Things Happen to Good People*.[4] Rabbi Kushner knew tragedy. He lost a son to illness. Anyone could understand why he would struggle with pain and questions, and he should be commended for his sincere, heartfelt effort to help hurting people answer tough questions. The answers he suggests, though, would not be comforting to many Christians. He says that if the world is not perfect, then God must not be perfect, and that however much God may want to get rid of evil, he must not have the ability to do so.[5] Kushner writes, "I can worship a God who hates suffering but cannot eliminate it, more easily than I can worship a God who chooses to make children suffer and die, for whatever exalted reason."[6] Ultimately, Kushner concludes, we just have to forgive God for not being perfect and for not making a perfect world.[7]

Us, forgive God? That's exactly backwards.

God, not perfect? That isn't what the Bible says at all, and it really doesn't make me feel any better about suffering to think of a god who is supposedly unable to help. To put it in Kushner's terms, I can worship a God whose ways I do not completely understand far more easily than I can worship a helpless god. In fact, if I *did* understand everything about God, what kind of God would that be?

That said—and this is important—it does not matter one whit what kind of God we prefer, or who we wish he was, or what we happen to find attractive in a deity. God is who he is, whether we like it or not.

I don't mean to suggest that it is wrong for C. S. Lewis or Rabbi Kushner (or you and me) to wrestle with these issues and offer theories. It is really important for some people to sort out how God and pain fit together. But theories are all they can ever be. We'll find out in heaven who (if anyone) was right. Spend a lifetime demanding that God defend himself, though, and a person will find it hard to be close to God.

"Pardon me, my lord," Gideon replied, "but if the LORD is with us, why has all this happened to us?" (Judg. 6:13)

4

Sometimes our question isn't about why suffering happens—why evil exists in the first place—but about the way it is spread around. We don't wonder so much about the presence of pain, but its allocation: Why him and not her? Or, why me and not someone else?

These questions are not answered in the Bible, either, and this study of the Bible's view of suffering is not going to attempt to answer the "why me" questions. If no one has found an answer by now, I don't think it's coming, so my focus is on the utility of the questions, not the various proposed answers.

But I was looking for answers, you say? So was Job. He didn't find them, either—at least not the ones he thought he wanted.

Job, remember, has questions. Not curses, but questions. Oh, his wife sings a different tune: "Are you still maintaining your integrity? Curse God and die!" (Job 2:9). *Thanks, honey.* But Job doesn't curse God. He just doesn't understand.

Enter Job's friends—Eliphaz, Bildad, and Zophar. For seven days, they truly are friends. They sit with Job in silence "because they saw how great his suffering was" (Job 2:13). But then they open their mouths, and there is a sharp drop in their utility.

"It's your fault, Job," they say. "We don't know what you did, but it must have been a doozy. You must have committed some terrible sin to be suffering this way." They take turns, three shots each, trying to convince Job that he is to blame. Now, sin does have consequences, and a difficult truth of Scripture is that sometimes we suffer the results of our sin even if we are forgiven. What foolishness, though, to suggest that personal sin is the *only* reason for suffering, or that we could possibly know when it is so.

Job responds with sarcasm. "I'm sure you speak for all the experts, and when you die there'll be no one left to tell us how to live" (Job 12:2 *The Message*). And he defends himself: "I will never admit you are in the right; till I die, I will not deny my integrity" (Job 27:5).

This leads Job to the *why me* question as he asks God, "Does it please you to oppress me, to spurn the work of your hands, while you smile on the plans of the wicked?" (Job 10:3).

And Job wonders how God could do this to him. He says, "I cry to you for help and you do not answer me; I stand, and you only look at me.

WHY ME? (And Why That's the Wrong Question)

You have turned cruel to me; with the might of your hand you persecute me" (Job 30:20–21 ESV).

What Job would really like is a chance to talk to God face-to-face about his suffering, but he knows he cannot. Job says:

> He is not a mere mortal like me that I might answer him, that we might confront each other in court. If only there were someone to mediate between us, someone to bring us together, someone to remove God's rod from me, so that his terror would frighten me no more. Then I would speak up without fear of him, but as it now stands with me, I cannot. (Job 9:32–35)

(Did you catch the part where Job sees that he needs someone between God and him? Job is recognizing the need for Jesus centuries before Jesus was born.)

Then, in a be-careful-what-you-wish-for moment, God shows up in a whirlwind to answer Job's call, if not his questions. God says, "Brace yourself like a man; I will question you, and you shall answer me" (Job 38:3).

Put on your big-boy pants, Job. Let's chat.

God's "answer" to Job's questions, it turns out, is to remind Job of who God is and who Job is not:

> Where were you when I laid the earth's foundation?
> Tell me, if you understand.
> Who marked off its dimensions? Surely you know!
> Who stretched a measuring line across it?
> On what were its footings set,
> or who laid its cornerstone—
> while the morning stars sang together
> and all the angels shouted for joy?
> Who shut up the sea behind doors
> when it burst forth from the womb,
> when I made the clouds its garment

and wrapped it in thick darkness,
when I fixed limits for it
and set its doors and bars in place,
when I said, 'This far you may come and no farther;
here is where your proud waves halt'? (Job 38:4–11)

Whoa. How do you respond to that? If you are as smart as Job, you'll say, *Okay, I'll shut up now*: "I am unworthy—how can I reply to you? I put my hand over my mouth" (Job 40:4).

My God, my God, why have you forsaken me? (Ps. 22:1)

5

So what can we take from the story of Job, with respect to the question of why suffering exists or why certain people seem to suffer more than others? I think one lesson of Job is that *we are not meant to know the entire answer to those questions.*

The truth is, there may be many possible reasons for our suffering, and, like Job, we probably will not learn in this life the specific reason that something bad has happened to us. Sometimes we suffer for our own sin, the natural consequences of reckless behavior. If you drive drunk and have an accident, there is no need to search the cosmos for a mystical reason for your suffering. Sometimes we suffer for someone else's sin, as when a spouse cheats, an addict drives a family to financial ruin, or a criminal commits a crime. Sometimes we are disciplined by God, as the Israelites were many times in the Old Testament. Sometimes we are pruned, as God molds our character.

There is enormous disagreement, incidentally, about whether God *causes* suffering or merely *allows* it to occur. Some say that God is a God of love and would never cause anyone to do evil. Others say God is completely sovereign and that nothing, absolutely nothing, not even a tragedy, happens that is outside his will. Faithful Christians will disagree on this point until it is answered in heaven. As for me, I don't think it denies God's sovereignty to believe that he allows us to have choices, and allows us to live with the consequences of those choices, but this debate is far beyond the scope of our discussion. This study does not attempt to join the scores of books looking for answers to such questions; instead, it is about whether it makes sense to dwell on such issues rather than focusing on God's glory and the results of our trials.

So it may be our own fault, it may be someone else's fault, it may be sent by God or permitted by God, or we may simply have bumped our head out of clumsiness and there is no grand cosmic reason for our suffering. Many times—maybe most times—we will never know the specific cause for specific suffering.

After all, if we were ever going to get the answer to the "why me" questions from the only authoritative source, the book of Job would have been it. Job was a godly man who got to hear the voice of God on the subject directly. It was the perfect opportunity for all involved. But as we saw above, God does not say, *Well, Job, you see Satan and I were talking about you one day, and....* He does not say that Job suffered for someone else's good, or to refine Job's character. He did not even say whether it was because of some sin in Job's life, which Job and his "friends" had been arguing about for thirty-something chapters. Instead, God says: *Okay ... everyone who created the universe and keeps it going, raise your hand. What's that, Job? Your hand's not up?*

Perhaps the issue cannot be reduced to a simple answer that can be understood by humans. Maybe God, for his own reasons, chooses not to explain all of life's mysteries to his creation. For whatever reason, he did not give us the answer to the "why me" question in Job.

Which means we probably are not ever going to get it, at least not in this life.

Which means we have to trust God.

Which may just be the point.

Who can fathom the Spirit of the LORD, or instruct the LORD as his counselor? Whom did the LORD consult to enlighten him, and who taught him the right way? Who was it that taught him knowledge, or showed him the path of understanding? (Isa. 40:13–14)

6

I don't know if my Uncle Joe's accident was exceptionally bad luck or if it was part of God's plan. I never will know, not until heaven, and even if I did know, it wouldn't bring him back. If I heard God's voice on the subject, his answer to me would likely be what it was to Job, a reminder of who is God and who isn't.

God took Job on a journey through nature. It's remarkable, it's miraculous what God does in ordering the universe. If he can take care of all that, can he not take care of our lives? How much do we trust the God who made us?

Because that is all that is left for Job to do: to trust. Job asked his questions to God directly, and God answered directly, and God's answer is . . . *himself*. Period.

Another truth Job teaches us is that it is pointless to speculate about why someone *else* is hurting. We are supposed to take care of people in pain, not waste time wondering about its cause. It's none of our business, and if God is not likely to explain it in those terms to the person doing the suffering, he sure isn't going to explain it to gossiping busybodies. As Gregory Boyd puts it, our job description "involves very little knowing but a great deal of loving."[8]

It does not mean that we won't still ask, like Job, *Why have you made me your target?* I don't think we ever will stop having those questions until we get to heaven. In fact, I think God knows it is our nature to ask those questions, and he wants us to take them to him, or else he wouldn't have recorded so many people asking the "why me" questions in the Bible.

And to the throne of God is *exactly* where we should take them. God never chastises Job for asking, and I think he'll understand if you ask, too. Just don't expect a direct answer to why you are suffering, or why some people seem to suffer more than others. Job did not get those answers, and I am not aware of anyone who ever has.

However, even if God chooses not to explain everything to us, he will walk with us through the trial, whatever its reason and whatever its source, and use it for good. That's if we get past the wrong questions and on to the right ones.

Notes

1. Why do people try to one-up each other with trials? In a class I taught long ago, there were two families constantly trying to outdo each other with tales of woe. We called it *prayer-request poker*: "I'll see your sick child and raise you a mother-in-law's knee surgery."

2. C. S. Lewis, *The Problem of Pain* (New York: HarperCollins, 1940), 24–25.

3. Gottfried Leibniz, *Essais de Théodicée sur la bonté de Dieu, la liberté de l'homme et l'origine du mal* [Essays on the goodness of god, the freedom of man and the origin of evil], trans. E. M. Huggard (Peru, IL: Open Court, 1985).

4. Harold S. Kushner, *When Bad Things Happen to Good People* (New York: Random House, 2001).

5. Ibid., 60–62, 79, 173.

6. Ibid., 180.

7. Ibid., 198.

8. Gregory Boyd, *Is God to Blame?* (Downers Grove, IL: InterVarsity, 2003), 104.

Chapter 2

THE ROOT OF OUR QUESTIONS

Like a tornado, trouble can come suddenly and seem random. It's human nature to wonder why a storm strikes here and not there. Because of our selfishness, pride, and desire for control over our lives, we do not simply regret pain; we are offended by it. But even in the aftermath of a tornado, we can see God's hand at work and the benefits of moving toward God-centered questions.

1

"We will keep an eye on it in coming days," the weatherman said.

It was Wednesday, April 20, 2011. They were watching a potential powerhouse storm system expected to reach Alabama a week later.

As the days passed, the models showed factors coming together in a scary way. Lower winds out of the south to bring in warm, humid air from the Gulf of Mexico. Cool air in the upper atmosphere. High wind shear. A perfect setup for supercell thunderstorms and damaging, long-track tornadoes.

WHY ME? (And Why That's the Wrong Question)

We heard these predictions for days. But it was April in Alabama. Tornado season. Stormy predictions were the norm. Besides, this was all a worst-case scenario, and those hardly ever come true.

This time, it did.

Around three o'clock in the afternoon on April 27, one of the first of many tornadoes plowed through Cullman, Alabama. We saw amazing images of the twister approaching downtown. There was extensive property damage, but miraculously only two deaths.

At almost exactly the same time, far from any television cameras, an F5 tornado hit the tiny town of Hackleburg, killing twenty-four people. It continued a dozen miles to Phil Campbell, where another twenty-six died. The winds were so strong that the storm lifted asphalt off the roads.

Then, around five o'clock, the weather service issued a tornado warning for Tuscaloosa. We were glued to the television by then (at least those of us who still had a roof and electricity). Schools let out early, sirens were sounding continuously, and reports were coming in of damage around the state. The channel we were watching had its rooftop cameras in Tuscaloosa pointed toward an ominous cloud in the west.

As the cloud got closer to the cameras, it became clear that this was no ordinary wall cloud. We were actually witnessing a nearly mile-wide tornado approach the city. On it came, crossing the interstate, lit up by power flashes as it tore through utility lines. We watched silently as it passed near the stadium and into subdivisions we knew well, through the student apartments, past the hospital and donut shop,[1] by the mall, and into the eastern neighborhoods. The cameras were too far away to see detailed damage, but we knew we were witnessing deaths. Thirty-nine in Tuscaloosa, it turns out.

The same tornado continued over the coal-mining region and into the northern Birmingham communities. Again, the funnel cloud was clearly visible from cameras atop Red Mountain. Twenty dead in Jefferson County.

Those were hardly the only storms of the day. Fifteen perished in St. Clair County, thirty-three in Fort Payne, nine in Cordova, and many more around the state. Over a four-day span, more than three hundred separate tornadoes killed 349 men, women, and children across the Southeast. From two-year-old Zy'Queria in Tuscaloosa, to eighty-six-year-old Oberia in Ashville, lives ended in a moment with a roar and a rush of two-hundred-miles-per-hour wind.

Not until the next day did we realize just how bad and widespread the damage was. Entire families gone, or perhaps even worse, only one left to mourn. The death counts were staggering, initially overreported because the bodily destruction was so great that some were counted more than once. The cleanup lasted for months. Rebuilding will go on for years. Some of the emotional scars, though, will last forever.

And it was no doubt the same a month later when 138 died in a Joplin, Missouri, tornado. And it was no doubt the same months earlier when an earthquake and tsunami hit Japan, or when Hurricane Sandy devastated the Northeast, or when the Mississippi flooded out of its banks, or when the 2001 earthquake rocked Gujarat, India, or when countless other natural disasters devastated one part of the world or another.

How do you process something like this, when there is so much loss over such a wide area? The needs in a time like that are overwhelming. Thousands without water, power, or shelter. Severe injuries and more deaths than can be counted. Is all of this God's will?

Suddenly a mighty wind swept in from the desert and struck the four corners of the house. (Job 1:19)

2

Tornadoes are, in many ways, like most of the trouble that comes our way, and they can help us understand why we ask some of the questions we wonder about. First, tornadoes come unpredictably and with little warning. Through the advances of science, we have a little more warning for tornadoes than we used to, but still the speed at which a neighborhood can turn from peace to rubble is frightening. One moment things seem fine, the next we are at nature's mercy, and even the best forecasts are uncertain.

Second, even if we have warning, there is often little we can do. No one can change the path of a tornado. And some of the tornadoes that day were so powerful that even people who went through their tornado drills—lowest room in the house, away from windows—perished. There was simply nothing to do short of getting underground, or, in the case of a Tuscaloosa barbecue restaurant, taking refuge in a meat freezer.

Third, tornadoes come indiscriminately and without explanation. One town is destroyed, another untouched; one neighborhood is devastated, another passed by. Even one house may be spared when nothing is left but a pile of debris on either side. Did God decide who would die and who would not? On what possible basis?

A lot of other trials are the same: sudden, unavoidable, and with no apparent order. Much of the time there is no obvious reason why one person should get sick and another doesn't, why lightning struck here and not there. Sure, sometimes a problem can be linked to behavior, like lung cancer and smoking, but many times trouble comes uninvited and for no apparent reason.

This bugs us. A lot. Obviously, anyone who is not insane would prefer a trouble-free life. Pain hurts, after all. But our reaction to suffering goes way beyond a pain reflex, especially when it seems random or particularly undeserved. It angers us because we are fundamentally selfish and because we hate not being in control.

When I say that we ask questions out of selfishness, I do not mean that we should feel guilty any time we feel sadness or a sense of loss, or for asking about it. Of course we will feel sad and confused during a trial.

I point to our selfishness—mine, too—as a partial explanation for why we think that we should be excluded from suffering.

In our fallen nature, nothing is more important than our own well-being. Without God, our first (and sometimes only) thought is about our comfort. We are born that way. No one has to teach a baby to be selfish. We would not steal if we were not selfish. We would not envy or kill or look out for number one. And God would have no need to tell us to "honor one another before [o]urselves," (Rom. 12:10). People, though, "feel but the pain of their own bodies and mourn only for themselves" (Job 14:22).

Selfishly and pridefully, we think that we should be happy and comfortable at all times and that we somehow deserve a life that knows only prosperity. So when the trial comes, we feel like we have been singled out, and we feel we are not getting our fair share of life's goodies. Somehow, we got the idea that anytime we are in pain, we are being cheated.

Trouble also bothers us because we want to be in charge. In our minds, we do not need a God who insists on telling us what to do. We do not need anyone to be Lord of our lives, because *we* want to be lord of our lives. This need for control makes us cringe whenever someone gets something we think they don't deserve, especially in America, with our culture of "rugged individualism" going back to pioneer days.

We have the idea that our future is whatever we make of it, that hard work will always pay off, and that everyone should make it on his own merit. It's the American Dream, and there is no room in the dream for a bolt from the blue that sends you back to square one when you've been doing your best. It simply does not fit with the way we think the world ought to be. (I'm not criticizing the American Dream. That kind of opportunity and freedom is one of the things that makes our country great. I simply offer it as another reason we expect to be in control and why, in turn, it disturbs us so much when trouble appears random.)

Is trouble arbitrary, outside of anyone's influence? Then we're not in control, and we hate it. Is everything ordained by God? Then we're not in control, and we hate it. Plus, if a person has bought into the theology that prosperity is always God's reward for good behavior, and adversity is always his punishment for bad behavior—a view that is not supported by Scripture—then every bruise will feel like judgment. No wonder we hate suffering if we struggle not only with the pain but also think it means we've done something wrong.

Because of our human nature, suffering doesn't just hurt; we are *offended* by it.

> No one knows when their hour will come: As fish are caught in a cruel net, or birds are taken in a snare, so men are trapped by evil times that fall unexpectedly upon them. (Eccles. 9:12)

3

In Alabama, we were offended by the tornadoes and wanted to know how God could let them happen. Why did they have to hit populated areas? Why did these families, these children, have to die? If Jesus calmed storms in the Bible, why not stop a couple of these? And of course, if we were one of the ones whose homes floated, slid, burned, or blew away, we asked, "Why me?"

But where do these questions get us? If we could find answers, that would be one thing, but (as we saw in the previous chapter) mankind has struggled with these questions since at least the time of Job, and we are no closer to finding answers now than we were then. If wrestling with the questions gave us any practical help, that too would be one thing, but it rarely benefits us or anyone else. We can ask those questions until we are blue in the face and, even if we knew the answers, it would not pick up one piece of rubble in Pratt City. It would not provide shelter for a single family or give one mom the disposable diapers she needs.

There are, however, some questions we can ask about suffering that *will* give us practical help, questions that *can* be answered. Ask how God can be glorified through the tornadoes, and you might notice a *New York Times* article about a welder in Cottondale, near Tuscaloosa, who was working out of state when the tornado hit his family's home. His wife and two young children sought shelter in the relatively sturdy hospital and were unharmed. Although they lost all their possessions, the article quotes the family as saying how they are "blessed" and how they did not lose the things that really matter.[2] Intentionally or not, because of the tornadoes, the *New York Times* shared the gospel with the entire world.

Ask how suffering might bring people closer to God, and you might think of worship services at Rosedale Baptist Church in Tuscaloosa, the first Sunday after the storm. The church lost its steeple, most of its roof, and much of its congregation, but not its spirit. The outdoor service was a refuge and a place of celebration amid little colored plastic flags marking where body parts were found. One hundred members and guests sang "Victory in Jesus" in the newly-calm open air.[3]

Ask how you can minister to people in need, and you will be nearly overwhelmed with opportunities to serve. People gathered from across the Southeast to help any way they could. Trucks set up in hundreds of locations to collect water, canned goods, clothes, and all sorts of needed supplies, hoping that people would be moved to help.

And were they ever. At least in the initial days after the destruction, trucks overflowed with donated goods. Organizations, faith based and secular, arrived in force to help with cleanup. Individuals came to designated checkpoints to volunteer their time. Restaurants found a way to open and give away food and ice. As one editorial put it, "We may have stumbled, but we will not fall, for we live in a community that believes in helping thy neighbor—and strangers, too."[4]

One of those persons moved to help was Holly Hart. An avid fan of the Auburn Tigers, Holly was not going to let a football rivalry stop her from ministering to storm victims in Tuscaloosa, the home of the Crimson Tide. Holly and a group of friends started "Toomer's for Tuscaloosa" and sent truck after truck of supplies, following in

WHY ME? (And Why That's the Wrong Question)

one simple motto: "We believe in the kindness of the human spirit, the importance of the human touch, and the strength that lies in each and every person." With the organization and Facebook page in place, Toomer's for Tuscaloosa later branched out to aid other communities in other disasters, from Arkansas to Georgia to Missouri. After the next disaster, whenever or wherever it may be, Holly and Toomer's for Tuscaloosa will be there.[5]

Maybe one of Holly's trucks brought supplies to Carson Tinker, a long snapper for the Crimson Tide. Carson worked with his teammates to help with the recovery, but he also felt the storm's effects up close and personal. As the tornado passed over student apartments, Carson held on tight to his girlfriend. Their apartment crumbling around them, the wind snatched Ashley from Carson's arms. Carson survived, but Ashley did not.

How do you turn the grief Carson felt into a spirit of giving? How do you stop thinking just about yourself and include others in your concern? According to Carson, it is a choice. "We didn't choose the circumstances that we went through," he said, "but we did choose how we responded."[6]

The rain came down, the streams rose, and the winds blew and beat against that house; yet it did not fall, because it had its foundation on the rock. (Matt. 7:25)

4

A few days after the tornadoes, my wife and son and I went shopping for relief supplies to take to one of the pickup points. The store was full of other families moved to do the same. Here were people driven to think beyond themselves, to just love someone else who was hurting, in a blast of love that would not have occurred without a blast of wind.

The young woman who checked us out was from Concord, a community that knows about tornadoes. Concord was hit in 2011, but it had also been devastated by an F5 tornado in April 1998.

Kathy looked tired, so tired, as she ran our items through the register. We asked, "Long day?"

"You might say that," she answered with a weary smile, and she explained how she had spent the day working in a relief shelter in her hometown before starting her evening shift.

"We lost our house back in '98," she said. "I remember how many people came through for us back then. It's funny: I was handing out water bottles today to some of the very same people who gave me water over ten years ago when I was in their shoes."

Kathy is someone who has learned to ask the right questions.

Notes

1. I often rode my bike to that donut shop in college. For less than a dollar, you could get a hot glazed donut and half a pint of milk. For some reason, I gained weight in college.

2. Dan Barry, "Losing Everything, Except What Really Matters," *New York Times*, April 30, 2011, www.nytimes.com/2011/05/01/us/01land.html?pagewanted=all.

3. Izzy Gould, "Tuscaloosa Pastor Encourages Flock at Outdoor Sunday Service, the First after Tornado," *Huntsville Times*, May 1, 2011, http://blog.al.com/live/2011/05/tuscaloosa_pastor_encourages_f.html?mobRedir=false.

4. John Peck and Mike Hollis, "Madison County Tornadoes: We Are Neighbors, All of Us," *Huntsville Times*, May 1, 2011, http://blog.al.com/breaking/2011/05/madison_county_tornadoes_we_ar.html?mobRedir=false.

5. Kim Cross, "What Stands in a Storm, Part III: Fellowship," *Southern Living*, August 2011, www.southernliving.com/general/tornado-stories-what-stands-in-a-storm-fellowship-00417000074347; http://ToomersforTuscaloosa.com; www.facebook.com/toomersfortuscaloosa.

6. Tommy Hicks, "Carson Tinker Belongs among Heroes—And Not Just the Sports Kind," *Mobile Press-Register*, December 9, 2011, www.al.com/sports/index.ssf/2011/12/carson_tinker_belongs_among_he.html.

MIKE & MIKE (1)

Allow me to introduce two guys I admire very much: Mike Reed and Mike Worley. Both learned that they had cancer, Mike Reed (Hodgkin's lymphoma) in 1999, when he was twenty years old, and Mike Worley (multiple myeloma) in 2011, when in his forties. There are two other things the Mikes have in common, and these things helped them during their battles with the disease: both were men of God, and both were married to godly women.

Mike and April Reed, and Mike and Pam Worley, are heroes of mine for the way they responded to their trials, but I bet they would be uncomfortable with me saying that. They would probably tell you that they had nothing to do with it, that God was at all times giving them strength. I have no doubt that is true, but they made the *choice* to let God give them strength. They made the *choice* not to let cancer distance them from God and make them bitter. Oh, I'm sure that at times they dealt with anger and disappointment, but I am also sure that when they felt that way, they took their honest feelings to God and did not dwell on them. They may occasionally have been tempted to ask, "Why me?" But they were more concerned that God be glorified however God chose to deal with their bodies.

I am going to let April (and sometimes Mike R.) and Pam tell their stories through their Caringbridge.com journals (which they were gracious enough to allow me to use—for *your* benefit, and to glorify God). When I first talked to Pam about using the Worley family's story, she said one of the reasons she wrote publicly was so that God would be glorified, whatever happens. When I talked to Mike and April about using their story, Mike said, "For others to benefit from our story is a blessing to us." Already you can see that their faith and courage will be an inspiration.

We will revisit them throughout the book. By the time we begin in 2010, Mike Reed is ten years into his battle, and Mike Worley has no idea what the next year has in store for him. Then following along in 2011, it is amazing to me how these families dealt with issues so similarly, at about the same time, even though to the best of my knowledge they have never met.

You will see that God was working in both families' lives, just not in the same way.

Reed

Monday, June 15, 2009, 5:30 PM (April)

I could never be an oncologist. I can't imagine how hard it was for Dr. M to look at us {Mike, almost 30 years old, fighting cancer for almost 10 years—1/3 of his life, a 5 month-old baby, etc.} and tell us that the PET scan did not look good. . . . There is a huge mass/cluster on his back/spine. It's a miracle that he's just now in pain. There's also a new node in his neck. The other lymph nodes in his chest and abdomen are about the same or a little worse.

Mike is okay. He handled the news well, as always. It's probably the reason he's managed to live a normal life with cancer for almost 10 years; he has faith and doesn't get discouraged easily.

Friday, June 19, 2009, 9:20 AM (April)

While we believe God could cure Mike any way He wishes, we've been told by numerous doctors that chemo will not cure Mike. We use chemo to keep the disease "in check" until he can start a clinical trial that has the potential to put him into remission.

Saturday, August 29, 2009, 8:07 AM (April)

BIG NEWS! Mike talked to his doctor yesterday and he told Mike that he can start the SGN-35 trial in less than a month!!!

Friday, February 11, 2011, 6:38 PM (April)

REMISSION! Dr. F called Mike and told him his PET scan was negative! He is in remission for the first time since 2003. Words can't describe our excitement. We are so incredibly thankful, and we know this was God's work.... Most people are amazed that Mike's been living with cancer for almost eight years. But our God is greater, stronger, and the ultimate physician.

Worley

Wednesday, April 6, 2011, 5:33 PM (Pam)

In September, Mike was getting a computer out of the car when he felt something in his back pop. He was in immediate pain and assumed he had pulled a muscle or thrown his back out. . . . Seven months after the initial injury, he was referred to a spine specialist. . . . He informed Mike that the cat scan showed a compression fracture on one of his vertebrae because of a cancer mass that was pushing against it. And there it was, the dreaded "C" word. . . . I can tell you that the next 24 hours were the worst ones I have ever spent! Mike and I talked (and cried) well into the night about our lives, our future, and how we wanted to handle it all. We decided that night our plan was (and still is), to handle everything with grace, dignity, joy, and thanksgiving.

The next day at 4:30 pm, we walked through the doors of Clearview Cancer Institute for the first time. You would think walking through those doors would be frightening and intimidating, but instead we felt an odd peace pour over us. That, my friends, is a peace that can be provided by only God himself!

Thursday, April 21, 2011, 5:35 PM (Pam)

We just got back from meeting with Dr. M getting the results from Mike's biopsy. I wish the news had been better than what we got, BUT it could be worse! Mike has multiple myeloma. It is a cancer of the plasma in the bone marrow. . . . Chemotherapy will more than likely have to be done.

So now you know as much as we know. Well, actually we do know some other things. We know our God is bigger than any of the trials we go through! We know that we have an unbelievable support group of friends who are mighty prayer warriors! We know who we believe in, and that He will see us through the days and weeks ahead! . . . We will face each day with the strength He provides us and we will carry on. It's not going to be an easy road but I'm sure that the outcome will make us stronger than ever before!

Wednesday, May 4, 2011, 9:00 PM (Pam)

. . . I sometimes wonder how we went from one day talking about car pool, dinner plans, and where we were going on vacation, to stem cell transplants, ports, and chemo therapy. But I know the "how" or the "why" is just not important, it's not worth wasting my time on! What is important is living. Living in the present, not the past or the future. That is where I meet with God, in the present, and I wait upon Him.

The Reeds, who had been dealing with cancer for many years, got some great news near the beginning of 2011: remission, a cancer patient's favorite word! The doctors said, though, that chemotherapy is unlikely to do more than keep the cancer "in check." That was a blow, especially with a new baby, but Mike and April's ultimate hope is not in medicine. Of course, while their hope is in God, God works through doctors, too, so it was good news when Mike was approved for the SGN-35 study, and *great* news when it showed promise.

This news was reason for praise. But pay attention to the way Mike and April did not reserve their praise for good news. They chose to have an attitude of praise throughout. Whatever their doctors told them, Mike and April turned to God with reverence and awe and faith. Whatever their doctors told them, Mike and April loved God, and they knew that God loved them.

Then just a few weeks after the Reeds learned of remission, the Worleys learned of Mike's cancer. Like the Reeds, Mike and Pam Worley are determined to be faithful no matter what is in store. Mike and Pam decided at the beginning—they made a choice—to respond well.

You can tell as you read their entries that these families did not wait for bad news to get to know God. When they started their journey, they already had a relationship with Jesus Christ and a habit of leaning on him no matter their circumstances. I bet they would tell you that is the reason they could handle this news in stride. Cancer did not rock their faith; cancer *strengthened* their faith.

Both families are asking the same questions. How can God be glorified? How is this going to strengthen our family and our relationship with God? What good is going to come out of this, whatever course the cancer ultimately takes? While they pray for healing, as they should, the questions they are asking do not deal only with their circumstances.

As we prepare to study the questions people ask during suffering, do you think that you would ask the same questions the Reeds and the Worleys are asking? Would you be able to respond as they have? Do you have the same faith and dependence on God that they have?

Would you like to?

PART TWO

The Wrong Questions

Chapter 3

WHY ME?
(Because Everyone Hurts)

When we ask *why me,* we assume that trouble happens to some people but not others. Reality says otherwise. The Bible and our own eyes tell us that *everyone* suffers in this life.

1
One fire, maybe. But two?

Many years ago, just after their son was born, some friends lost their home in a fire. No one was at home and no one was injured, so they had much to be grateful for, but it was still a tremendous blow. They suffered the loss of irreplaceable photographs and the displacement of hotel and apartment living (with an infant!) while the home was being rebuilt.

As the new house neared completion and our friends prepared to return to normalcy, it burned down. Again. Sometimes, I suppose, lightning *does* strike twice.

In the world you will have much trouble. (John 16:33 NLV)

2

What did you expect?

Did you really think you would get through this life without pain? Or did you think that if you became a Christian, all of your troubles would suddenly vanish?

Nope. God never promised that this life would be just like heaven. That comes later. For now, we are stuck in the same world as everyone else, and as long as we are alive, there will be heartache, sorrow, and tragedy. There will also be good times, sure, but let's dispel the notion right now that anyone is immune from trouble just for being "good," or for being a follower of Jesus, or for being anything.

Since I started paying attention to the questions people ask about suffering, the one I heard more than any other is "why me?" When bad stuff happens, people feel singled out somehow, as if their experience is different from anyone else's, as if no one has ever known pain like they have. And usually, if we're honest, we ask that question because we believe that there is some kind of inherent goodness within that has earned us a pass from the kind of suffering other people face. In reality, though, there is nothing we face that others haven't faced before. Granted, that fact doesn't mean our pain isn't real, and it truly may be that the average person does not face the same kind of trial that we are facing. But if we expect to make it through this world without suffering, we'd best get used to disappointment. And if we think that being good will eliminate pain from our journey, we'd best read our Bibles.

Do not believe what you sometimes hear, that if you become a Christian and have enough faith, all your worldly troubles will end. It isn't biblical. It isn't true. God never promised that he would always answer prayer in exactly the way we want. He never said following him will excuse you from the laws of physics or eliminate the everyday hassles of living.

Think of it this way: If being a "good Christian" guaranteed a good time, then Jesus must have had a breeze of a life, right? Hardly. In fact, if we are honest, our suffering does not compare to what Jesus went through, and he was *perfect*.

> *He was despised and rejected by mankind, a man of suffering, and familiar with pain. Like one from whom people hide their faces he was despised, and we held him in low esteem. (Isa. 53:3)*

3

Is your trial being made fun of? Misunderstood? Jesus was, too. Born less than nine months after the wedding, the whispers and taunts must have started early for Jesus. Then, once he began his ministry, even his half-brothers rejected him and were, it seems, a little embarrassed. *Hey, Jesus. It's great, your preaching here in our hometown and all. But you know what you ought to do? Take your message to the Judeans! Why don't you try it out there where our friends don't have to hear it? Need help packing?* (John 7:3–5). He was mocked until the day he died—literally.

Got money problems? Jesus was *homeless*. "Foxes have dens and birds have nests," Jesus told one shallow recruit, "but the Son of Man has no place to lay his head" (Matt. 8:20).

Are you lonely? When Jesus needed them most, his closest followers slept, ran away, betrayed him, and denied even knowing him (Mark 14:37–72).

Are your children rebellious and frustrating? Read the Gospels and see how slow the Keystone Cop disciples were to grasp his message. (Actually, all I have to do is look in the mirror to see that Jesus has to put up with a frustrating and rebellious child.)

Struggling with temptation? Jesus faced all the same temptations that we face. No, he did not give in, but he faced them just like you and I (Heb. 2:17–18; 4:15).

Are you grieving? Jesus grieved when he learned that his cousin John the Baptist had been shortened by a head (Matt. 14:10–14). He wept when his friend Lazarus died (John 11:35). And he grieved for his stubborn people, too proud to enter into his love, saying that he longed to gather them the way a hen gathers her chicks (Matt. 23:37).

Physical pain? Jesus was beaten with a rod and lashed with a whip. He wore a crown of thorns that was pounded into his scalp. Then he was nailed to the cross through his wrists and feet, bearing his weight on his arms so that he would have to push himself up, rubbing his bloodied back against the rough wood just to take a breath.

Or maybe you have been told that you only have a few months to live. Jesus was, too. His entire life led to the cross, and he knew it. He tried and tried to explain to the disciples that "the Son of Man"—that's what Jesus liked to call himself—"is going to be delivered into the hands of men. They will kill him, and on the third day he will be raised to life" (Matt. 17:22–23). Try living your whole life knowing you are going to die a painful, violent death as a young man.

Feel distant from God? In spite of all else that Jesus went through, the suffering that hurt him the most may have been when he was separated from God. On the cross, he became sin so that we might become righteousness. God, who is perfectly holy, cannot tolerate sin. Taking on our sin separated the Son from the Father for that time. Hear Jesus' anguish when he cries, "My God, my God, why have you forsaken me?" (Matt. 27:46).

Jesus, you see, went through all that we do, and more. That does not mean our pain isn't real, but it does mean at least this: it is silly to think that trying to live a good life will let us escape suffering, when the only perfect man who ever lived suffered more than anyone.

For sighing has become my daily food;
my groans pour out like water. (Job 3:24)

4

It's hard to reconcile large-scale disasters with our assumption that anyone—even "good" people—can get through life without suffering. The oil spill in the Gulf of Mexico a few years ago is a perfect example.

On April 20, 2010, at 9:45 in the evening, a pocket of methane gas shot through the drill column of the Deepwater Horizon oil rig in the Gulf of Mexico and exploded. Most workers on the oil rig escaped, but eleven were never found.

The blast was only the beginning. Two days later, an oil slick appeared at the site of the explosion. For months, thousands of barrels of oil leaked daily into the Gulf. Wind and currents pushed the slick north and east, and in June, oil and tar balls began washing up on beaches from Louisiana to Pensacola.

The whole country was watching, including thousands who had planned beach vacations. Many cancelled or moved their reservations to another beach. I know, I know: missing a beach vacation doesn't seem like much of a tragedy. Think for a minute, though, about what all those cancellations did to the natives.

Orange Beach, Alabama, is a tourist town, and many people hope to make 90 percent of their income during the summer months. The spill could not have happened at a worse time. People cancelled their vacations left and right, and that summer Orange Beach resembled a ghost town more than a tourist attraction.

Restaurants cut back to winter staff, so some servers, bartenders, and busboys lost their jobs altogether. Others kept their jobs, but tips were a quarter or less of what they had been in previous summers. Hotels that hired extra maids for the summer let half of them go because the rooms were empty and did not need to be cleaned. The gulf waters were closed to fishing, so the captains, the deckhands, and the ex-hippie who ran the bait shop all had to go without paychecks.

The lady who owns the photography studio; Carl, who was getting ready to open a new snack bar; the pastor's wife with the consignment shop in Foley; A. J., the seventy-two-year-old handyman who lost the contract with a major rental company; Mark, the bartender who moved here so that he and his pregnant fiancée could scrape up enough money to get their own place; Gladys, the recently-widowed grandmother whose retirement is tied up in rental properties and had *every single* reservation for the summer cancelled—they all had their feet cut out from under them.

I met these people, and many more, through my work. The fear in their eyes was heartbreaking, and there was nothing we could do to make their lives "normal" again. A lot of people got checks, but not enough to cover all the costs, and money does not solve everything. It certainly did not make up for the loss of pride for people who just wanted to work and didn't know what to do next. Many wondered if they should just pull up stakes and try it somewhere else, because no one knew how long the oil would flow or how long the guests would stay away. At the time, there was real concern that a way of life was simply over. People were scared, desperate, and alone.

The environmental and economic damage caused by the oil spill was region-wide. It did not affect only the good, or the bad, or the indifferent. The fear and desperation were everywhere, and the people there did not do anything to bring it on themselves. All they did was live and work in a town that got in the way of a man-made disaster through no fault of their own.

I am worn out from my groaning. All night long I flood my bed with weeping and drench my couch with tears. (Ps. 6:6)

5

Trouble can seem completely random. The wildfire destroys one house and skips another, the lifelong jogger dies of heart failure, and the stray bullet hits an innocent bystander and not the person next to him. Even with a large-scale disaster, like a hurricane or an oil spill, that affects everyone in a particular area, had there been a slight shift of wind or current, an entirely different area would have suffered the worst of the damage.

Maybe a particular *kind* of trouble seems random, but trouble itself is not. It is universal. You may not know what kind of storms you will have to contend with in life, but storms will come. We *know* this, yet we continually act surprised, offended even, as if God had guaranteed us a trouble-free life. He did nothing of the sort.

Jesus said, "In this world you will have trouble" (John 16:33). Now, he follows that by telling us, "Take heart! I have overcome the world," but he could not be clearer: we *will* have trouble in this world. "Do not be surprised," Peter writes, "at the fiery ordeal that has come on you to test you, as though something strange were happening to you" (1 Pet. 4:12). Pain and death are simply part of the human condition.

It was not always so. God created a world without pain, without sorrow, without death, and without heartache. Adam and Eve had perfect union with him, but that wasn't good enough, and they sinned. Oh, God warned them: "You are free to eat from any tree in the garden; but you must not eat from the tree of the knowledge of good and evil, for when you eat from it you will certainly die" (Gen. 2:16–17). But they sinned anyway, and just as God said, it led to death: "Sin entered the world through one man, and death through sin, and in this way death came to all people, because all sinned" (Rom. 5:12).

Everything changed. The people were kicked out of Eden and separated from God; from that point on, childbirth and work were marked by pain (Gen. 3:16–19). And we have kept on sinning, kept on hurting, and kept on dying to this day.

The curse after the fall applies to us all, so we all suffer. We die, sooner or later. If we live long enough, we get old and deal with wrinkles, guts, hair loss, aches, and forgetfulness. We need a place to live, so we have to work, which is usually less fun than not working (although don't bother complaining about your job to someone out of work). We interact with people as human as we are, so we disappoint them and they disappoint us. No matter how good you try to be, no amount of trying will exempt you from the normal hassles of life.

I am feeble and utterly crushed;
I groan in anguish of heart. (Ps. 38:8)

6

Nor will being a Christian free you from pain. As a matter of fact, the Bible says that believers will suffer in some ways that nonbelievers don't.

This is the inevitable consequence of living for Christ in a world that hates Christ, and the world does indeed hate Jesus. He is Lord, and we do not want anyone to be our lord. He is the light, and "everyone who does evil hates the light, and will not come into the light for fear that their deeds will be exposed" (John 3:20). "The world . . . hates me," Jesus said, "because I testify that its works are evil" (John 7:7).

If we live for Christ, the world will hate us, too. We should hope it is not because we are self-righteous and judgmental, but because we are living the gospel. If our faith can be seen by the way we think and live, we will be persecuted for our faith, as Jesus warned his disciples: "If the world hates you, keep in mind that it hated me first. If you belonged to the world, it would love you as its own. As it is, you do not belong to the world, but I have chosen you out of the world. That is why the world hates you" (John 15:18–19).

Paul likewise warned his readers that hurting is part of the believer's job description. He wrote to Timothy that "all who desire to live a godly life in Christ Jesus will be persecuted" (2 Tim. 3:12 ESV). He warned the people of Philippi that "it has been granted to you on behalf of Christ not only to believe in him, but also to suffer for him" (Phil. 1:29).

There are, of course, degrees of persecution. The disciples were martyred for their faith, and there are parts of the world where Christians are imprisoned, tortured, or even killed for professing Christ today. In the West, persecution is much more likely to take a different and less violent form. Perhaps we are simply excluded or judged. Admittedly, being made fun of is not even "suffering" compared to what some have gone through. Nonetheless, if we profess Christ as Lord, there will be persecution by the world, whether it is insignificant snickers or the ultimate loss of life.

All that to say this: Remember all the suffering that happens just by virtue of being part of the human race? Being a Christian only adds to that. Maybe a little, maybe a lot, but a follower of Jesus suffers in addition to the ways that the world suffers.

---

*People have heard my groaning,
but there is no one to comfort me. (Lam. 1:21)*

7

I am not trying to depress you. *Of course* there are wonderful parts of life. God blesses us in so many ways, and there is joy in a million unheralded daily moments. The sun rises, babies are born, and sometimes our relationships click. Most of us in this country—but certainly not all of us—know where the next meal is coming from and where we will sleep. We may be fortunate enough to have steady and rewarding work.

Jesus said he desires that our "joy may be complete" (John 15:11) and that we have "the full measure of [his] joy within [us]" (John 17:13). We can and should be grateful for the times when "our mouths were filled with laughter, our tongues with songs of joy" (Ps. 126:2).

It's not *all* bad, but we are not in Eden anymore, and "even in laughter the heart may ache" (Prov. 14:13). I will say it again: pain and death are a part of life. The good news is that it will not be like this forever.

First of all, trials are almost always temporary. A loss of employment can be scary and painful, but we usually find another job, sooner or later. The loss of a loved one is not something that ever goes away, but grief does wane in time. Peter said we would suffer "all kinds" of trials, but noted that it was for "a little while" (1 Pet. 1:6). Storms come; storms go.

Still, some storms last as long as this life. A person born with an incurable condition will suffer until she sleeps. A limb that is lost will not grow back. In a very, very important way, however, even these sufferings will not last forever. All trials, including the pain of death, are fleeting for the believer because one day God will make everything new: "See, I will create new heavens and a new earth. The former things will not be remembered, nor will they come to mind" (Isa. 65:17). On that day, God "will wipe every tear from [our] eyes. There will be no more death or mourning or crying or pain, for the old order of things has passed away" (Rev. 21:4).

How does that help me now, you ask? It helps by giving us hope, and it helps by giving us perspective. The hope is the promise of heaven. The promise does not take away today's pain, but it *can* help to know that our present trial is temporary and that a better day is coming. With the loss of a friend or family member, or in the case of our own pending death, it absolutely comforts us to know that death is not the end and that the believer will one day be reunited with his loved ones in Christ.

The perspective comes from realizing—to the extent our feeble human brains can wrap around perfection—just how great that day will be. The glories of eternity will make any thought of today's storm pass away: "I consider that our present sufferings are not worth comparing with the glory that will be revealed in us. For the creation waits in eager expectation for the children of God to be revealed" (Rom. 8:18–19).

Do you get that? The entire universe stands on tiptoe, waiting to see us glorified in eternity—waiting, as we are, for God to make everything right.

(But note this: As great as the thought of heaven is, it isn't true that the only way we can make it through suffering is to think of eternity to come, when God will fix it all. It is a comfort, but as we will discuss in Part Three, suffering has benefits in the *present*, along with the pain. It's good news that our lives have purpose in spite of trials, but later chapters discuss even better news: Sometimes our trials give us purpose we would not otherwise have.)

You turned my wailing into dancing; you removed my sackcloth and clothed me with joy. (Ps. 30:11)

8

We had dinner recently with Ron and Jill, our friends whose house burned down, and then burned down again. We talked about that time long ago, when our sons were both young. As awful as it was, Ron says that their crisis was a turning point in his life. When our church reached out to him, he experienced God's love in a new way. Sure, it would have been great if it had never happened, but it *did* happen, and God used it for good.

Whether we like it or not, we're going to have pain in this world. In a way, it makes no sense to ask "why me" when everyone else is suffering, too. I admit that not all suffering is the same, of course. Not everyone loses a child. Not everyone dies in a car accident in their teens. Not everyone gets lupus, or multiple sclerosis, or cancer. Without a doubt, some people have a harder go of things than others, but still we all die, and we all hurt, and we all have some moments of joy. Suffering is natural and universal, but it still feels . . . *off*.

And it should. God set eternity in our hearts (Eccles. 3:11). At the level of our souls, we know that we were meant for another place. We know that there is something wrong with this world. It makes perfect sense that we would question the wrongness of it all. Still, we are wrong ourselves to think that God has somehow failed if every single person is not deliriously happy all the time. We are not yet to that part of the story.

To ask *why me* ignores what our eyes tell us: "Man is born to trouble as surely as sparks fly upward" (Job 5:7). Pain and sorrow, loss and heartache are universal conditions and no one gets a pass. Not the "good" people, not the bad, not anyone. God "causes his sun to rise on the evil and the good, and sends rain on the righteous and the unrighteous" (Matt. 5:45).

Chances are, as they say, you are already in a trial, you have just been through one, or one is headed your way. We do not have to live in fear, though, because we do not go through storms alone, and storms do not last forever.

I do not know how long it will take for there to be no trace of oil in the Gulf of Mexico or for the New Jersey coast to rebuild from Superstorm Sandy. Though that day will come, the people in the middle of a trial feel pain *now*. We should help and comfort where we can, and sometimes it will seem unfair from our human perspective.

For now, though, pain is a way of life. For everyone.

Chapter 4

WHY DO BAD THINGS HAPPEN TO GOOD PEOPLE? PART ONE

(What Good People?)

> We ask, "Why do bad things happen to good people?" The hard truth is that there are no good people, and we are not in a position to judge who deserves what kind of life.

1

I remember when seeing an old friend's name on caller ID meant good news, like an exciting job opportunity or a baby on the way. I'm getting to the age when the call is more often about a diagnosis.

Here is the news I have heard just in the recent past, and just about one specific kind of suffering: A family member's boss, father of two, has cancer in the marrow of his spine. A Sunday-school-class member, in remission, with a spot of uncertainty that showed up on the last scan. A college friend's wife, thyroid cancer, with a good prognosis, but still. A dear friend who was a bridesmaid in our wedding has breast cancer, back after apparent remission.

WHY ME? (And Why That's the Wrong Question)

All in a two-month span. Each in their late thirties to mid-forties. Churchgoers. Moms and dads, husbands and wives, people who love their families. People we would call "good." And those are just the people somehow connected to me in one little corner of the world.

Of course, the people in *my* life and *my* age group were not the only ones to get this kind of news. Around the same time, Willie Simmons Jackson died of cancer at the age of sixty. Back on July 5, 1987, in the small town of Elba, Alabama, Jackson used an antique iron, a pair of scissors, and a broken broom handle to murder eighty-seven-year-old Elmo Roberts for fifty-five dollars and a blank check. Jackson forged the check to buy a hamburger at a local Hardee's. Busted for the forgery, Jackson confessed to the murder and all its grisly details. He died in prison awaiting execution.

Do you think I felt the same way about Mr. Jackson's cancer as I did about that of my friends?

Do you think I should?

How long, Lord, will the wicked,
how long will the wicked be jubilant? (Ps. 94:3)

2

We don't respond the same when different people receive the same bad news. We tend to classify suffering by our opinion of the person doing the suffering. When people we label as "bad" are suffering, we think it is just. When people we label as "good" are suffering, we think it is unfair, it is a shame, it is tragic. We don't like it one bit. And we want to know just who God thinks he is to allow this sort of stuff to go on.

It is a question that a lot of people in the Bible ask: Why are good people suffering while bad people prosper?

- "How long will you defend the unjust and show partiality to the wicked?" (Ps. 82:2–4).
- "Why do you make me look at injustice? . . . Why are you silent while the wicked swallow up those more righteous than themselves?" (Hab. 1:3a; 13b).
- "Why do the wicked live on, growing old and increasing in power?" (Job 21:7).
- "Why does the way of the wicked prosper?" (Jer. 12:1b).
- "I have seen good people die in spite of their goodness and evil people live a long time in spite of their evil" (Eccles. 7:15 NCV).
- "Bad things happen to good people, and good things happen to bad people" (Eccles. 8:14a NCV).

You want to know the answer to these questions. So do I. Why do good people suffer? If we look to the Bible for answers, though, we find a very difficult truth to face: *there are no good people.*

There are people who are innocent, yes. When twenty first-graders died in a Connecticut elementary school, the sheer number of deaths was horrifying, but it was the innocent nature of the children that moved a nation to tears. And rightly so. Some situations just feel sadder than others, and I'm not suggesting that those families should not have received the outpouring of affection the public offered.

We don't reserve our judgment to innocent children, though. We tend to look at almost any suffering and judge whether it is deserved or undeserved, based on what we think of the victim. What gives us the right to decide who is good and who is bad, when like it or not, we're *all* bad?

*Everyone has turned away, all have become corrupt;
there is no one who does good, not even one. (Ps. 53:3)*

3

We think we know who the good and bad people are. We shake our heads at the death of a young man, or someone who has others depending upon her, although youth and responsibility do not make a person righteous.

We might say that bad people are those who *cause* suffering in others (a murderer), and good people are those who work to *reduce* suffering in others (Mother Teresa). Causing pain is certainly bad, and reducing suffering is a good thing to do, but does anyone really do all one or the other? Is there a criminal who does not have at least one act of kindness on his ledger?[1] And doesn't the most charitable person cause at least some pain at some point in her life?

What we really think is that the good people are those who do more good than bad overall, and bad people are those who do more bad than good. We picture a scale of justice weighing out a person's conduct, and a person is either good or bad depending upon which way the scale tips. And, we reason, if the scale tips on the side of goodness and virtue, that person should not have to suffer.

This is the way we think. This . . . is bad theology.

All of us have become like one who is unclean, and all our righteous acts are like filthy rags. (Isa. 64:6)

4

God does not judge the way we do. The God revealed in the Bible is perfect (2 Sam. 22:31). Being perfect, God's standard is himself, and to be righteous we must be exactly like him—utterly, completely, totally without sin of any kind: "Be perfect, therefore, as your heavenly Father is perfect" (Matt. 5:48). "Be holy, because I am holy" (Lev. 11:45b).

But it's not like I've murdered anybody, you say. Maybe not, but God does not rank sins the way we do. They are all equally serious, and damning, in his eyes. Any sin, no matter how minor we think it is, falls short of perfection, and we might as well have broken *all* the commandments (James 2:10).

What if I spend my whole life trying as hard as I can to be good, you ask? Well, you haven't (no one has), but even if you could put forth your best effort at all times, it wouldn't be perfect. It wouldn't be enough. Our best efforts are like garbage when weighed against God's standard (Isa. 64:6a).

So are you saying that no one *is good?* Yep. Because God said so, clearly, plainly, and leaving no room for debate: "Indeed, there is no one on earth who is righteous, no one who does what is right and never sins" (Eccles. 7:20). "For all have sinned and fall short of the glory of God" (Rom. 3:23).

I'm not crazy about it, either. My pride makes me want to be good on my own. I do not like being told that I cannot do it. But what I want and what I like does not change the truth: I am a sinner. We all are. We want to go our own way. We are prideful and stubborn and selfish. We are, simply, not perfect. And if we are not perfectly good, then we are rotten.

The next time you think that it would be great if God removed all evil from the world, stop to consider this: Would you be around the next day? I know I wouldn't.

If we claim we're free of sin, we're only fooling ourselves.
(1 John 1:8 The Message)

5

If God's standard is perfection, if none of us meets that standard, and if none of us is "good," what sense does it make to argue that this person is better than that person, or that this person "deserved" to suffer and that one did not? It makes no sense at all to sit on our pedestals and try to figure out who deserves what, when we all deserve hell.

As a matter of fact, God demonstrates his love, mercy, and goodness every single day that he does not blot mankind out of creation. "Because of the Lord's great love we are not consumed, for his compassions never fail" (Lam. 3:22). In his great mercy, he holds his wrath so that people might have the chance to turn to him: "As surely as I live, declares the Sovereign Lord, I take no pleasure in the death of the wicked, but rather that they turn from their ways and live" (Ezek. 33:11).

So no, we do not always get what we deserve, and we should be very, very grateful for that. I am not saying that the answer to suffering is self-disgust, and I certainly am not saying that we should say to someone in the midst of a trial, *So what? You are only getting what you had coming!* My point is this: by God's standards, none of us is better than anyone else. It is therefore a waste of time to try to sort out whose suffering is more or less "just." All suffering hurts, and our job is to love others through their pain, not to judge them.

We all, like sheep, have gone astray. (Isa. 53:6)

6

So how does anyone get to heaven? That is a pertinent question to our topic, because God's provision for our salvation gives us insight into his attitude toward our suffering. God could, justly, leave us in our sin and condemn everyone to hell. In his love, however, he provided a way. It is called the gospel—the *good news*.

We cannot live a perfect life, and our sin separates us from God. Jesus did live a perfect life (2 Cor. 5:21), and he died for our sins. "You see, at just the right time, when we were still powerless, Christ died for the ungodly" (Rom. 5:6).

Because he had no sin, when Jesus died he could take our punishment upon himself. (He had no sin to die for, and thus could die for ours.) "He himself bore our sins in his body on the cross, so that we might die to sins and live for righteousness; by his wounds you have been healed" (1 Pet. 2:24).

We know, by the evidence of the resurrection, that Jesus' sacrifice was acceptable to God. Therefore, if we put our faith in Jesus, if he is Lord and Savior, we are clothed with his righteousness (2 Cor. 5:21). He took on our sin, so that our own record of wrongdoing would not be held against us. That's good news, because if God kept score, we would lose every time: "If you, Lord, kept a record of sins, Lord, who could stand?" (Ps. 130:3).

The gospel is not the administration of *justice*, but of *grace*. We do not deserve to be saved, but through the cross, God saves us anyway. If you believe God takes pleasure in causing, or allowing, people to suffer, the gospel shows us that the exact opposite is true: he has gone out of his way to give us *good* things we do not deserve.

It is a hard truth to recognize that we each deserve hell. Once grasped, though, we realize that every breath is more than we deserve, that it is foolish to think that we can be "good" enough to earn a pain-free life, and that it is incredible that he offers forgiveness we could never earn.

Do you think that these Galileans were worse sinners than all the other Galileans because they suffered this way? (Luke 13:2)

7

The other side of the coin—and a mistake in its own right, made by Job's friends—is when we assume that if a person is suffering, he or she must have done something especially bad. We may wonder what someone did to invite karma's visit. The Bible refutes this notion, too.

Oh, there are certainly times in the Bible when God punishes or disciplines a people or an individual for sin. Consider Israel's time in Babylonian captivity (Jer. 25), or the grief David caused himself and his family by having an extramarital affair (2 Sam. 11–12). But what is *sometimes* true is not necessarily *always* true. As we learned from Job's story, not all suffering is a direct consequence of doing something bad. We should not assume it about ourselves, and we certainly should not assume it about others.

Jesus addressed this point directly in Luke's Gospel. Someone gave Jesus the harrowing news that Pilate, a Roman official, had murdered Galileans, their blood "mixed with their sacrifices" (Luke 13:1). The person telling the story, or someone in the crowd, jumped to the conclusion that the Galileans died because of sin in their life or because their sin was worse than others'. Jesus nipped that in the bud:

> Do you think that these Galileans were worse sinners than all the other Galileans because they suffered this way? I tell you, no! But unless you repent, you too will all perish. Or those eighteen who died when the tower in Siloam fell on them—do you think they were more guilty than all the others living in Jerusalem? I tell you, no! But unless you repent, you too will all perish. (Luke 13:2–5)

Do you think this terrible thing happened because the Galileans themselves were terrible? Or that eighteen victims of a construction accident were any guiltier than people who were not crushed? No! Why don't you worry more about your own sin instead of pointing fingers?

Jesus was emphatic with his response. An assumption that linked the tragedy to the guilt of the victim was not justified. All of Israel needed to repent, not just those standing beneath a faulty tower. All of Israel needed to believe in the Son who was sent, Jesus said, or they too would perish. And forty years after rejecting Jesus, Jerusalem fell and the temple was destroyed.

On another occasion, Jesus and his disciples came upon a blind man, and the disciples asked, "Rabbi, who sinned, this man or his parents, that he was born blind?" (John 9:2). The disciples were sure that the blindness was caused by sin, and the only question in their minds was whose sin it was. Jesus said, "Neither this man nor his parents sinned, but this happened so that the works of God might be displayed in him" (John 9:3).

Now, Jesus appears to say here that there was a planned purpose for the man's blindness, and it was so that God could be glorified, perhaps by the healing that is about to take place. That is, God decided that this man would be blind so that Jesus could come around later, heal him, and make God look good.

Maybe so, but according to Gregory Boyd, who has studied the passage in the original Greek, this is not the only translation that the original language supports. Jesus could also have said simply, "Neither this man nor his parents sinned; let God be glorified!"[2] *Don't worry yourself with the cause. It is what it is. Just let God be glorified by what I'm about to do.*

If Boyd is correct—I do not read Greek and cannot judge his claim—then *The Message* may have the right translation: "Jesus said, 'You're asking the wrong question. You're looking for someone to blame. There is no such cause-effect here. *Look instead for what God can do*'" (John 9:3 *The Message*; italics added).

Not every hardship is the consequence of specific sin, and we do not help the situation by trying to guess the cause of a trial. We are on shaky ground if we try to connect every injury to wrongdoing, because we are again putting ourselves in the seat of judgment and sorting out who deserves what. That is not our job.

"What did I do wrong?" we cry. Heaven cries back, "Everything, but I love you anyway. Always have, always will."[3]

8

About 144,000 people die every day. On August 31, 1997, one of those was Princess Diana of Wales, who died at the age of thirty-six in an automobile accident. Her death moved the world. She was a young, attractive, charismatic, and charitable mother of two, widely perceived as a victim in her divorce from the heir to the British throne—all the ingredients of what we consider an untimely and unfair passing. For months, thousands of people who had never met her brought flowers to memorial sites.

What about the other 143,999 people who died that day? Not to take anything away from Princess Di, but was she any better than anyone else who died? Better than Mother Teresa, who died one week later? What sense does it make to judge one death more tragic than another?

Through God's eyes, outside of the provision of the cross, there is no moral difference between me and a murderer on death row. (As a matter of fact, I was on eternal "death row" until I was saved.) What right then do I have to judge? Yet I do it every day. I judge others, when I think it is more suitable for one person to suffer than another. And I judge God, when I accuse him of not knowing what he is doing in allowing certain things to happen.

Of *course* I wish my friends did not have cancer, and it's natural that their suffering would impact me more than a stranger's. But is it right for me to think any one person deserves it more or less than another? The better attitude would be to hate it equally when any person has cancer, without regard to my flawed view of their relative moral worth.

The better attitude would be to stop judging who deserves what, when none of us deserve another heartbeat.

Notes

1. Spenser, my favorite fictional detective (in books by Robert B. Parker), makes this same point frequently by noting that Hitler liked dogs.
2. Gregory Boyd, *Is God to Blame?* (Downers Grove, IL: InterVarsity, 2003), 54–55.
3. Sheila Walsh, *Life Is Tough But God Is Faithful* (Nashville: Thomas Nelson, 1999), 23.

Chapter 5

WHY DO BAD THINGS HAPPEN TO GOOD PEOPLE? PART TWO

(Is it Really a "Bad" Thing?)

> We ask, "Why do bad things happen to good people?" That assumes that we can always tell what is good for a person and what is not. In fact, some of the things we complain about are for the best.

1

Maybe we were just too young.

After a few years practicing law at one of the largest firms in the state, I became the third lawyer at a firm with two other young attorneys. It was not an easy decision to leave the security of a larger firm. My wife and I were getting ready to start a family, though, and I had recently become more active in our church. I wanted to make a change so that I could be the kind of father I wanted to be and have more time to devote to ministry. So I joined Trip and Shelley and could not believe how family-friendly a small, youthful firm could be.

Things went great for a few years, but then the economics stopped working. It was no one's fault, and no one's failure, but it became clear that we couldn't wait for things to change. We had families to support. Our parting was reluctant and amicable, but disappointing to me. I felt like a failure. I had no idea where to go for a job and was scared for the future.

Mostly, though, I was confused. When I first made the jump to a smaller outfit, I firmly believed that I was following God's direction. *I must have misunderstood*, I thought. *God would never lead me to a dead end, would he?*

> *No eye has seen, no ear has heard, and no mind has imagined what God has prepared for those who love him. (1 Cor. 2:9 NLT)*

2

I'm not the only one who ever feared that God had steered him wrong.

For four centuries, the Israelites, enslaved by the Egyptians, cried out to God. They knew God had promised their ancestor Abraham that they would have a land of their own, the Promised Land. He didn't say when, though, and God had not mentioned a four-hundred-year detour of making bricks in the desert sun. But God heard the Israelites' prayers and said:

> I have indeed seen the misery of my people in Egypt. I have heard them crying out because of their slave drivers, and I am concerned about their suffering. So I have come down to rescue them from the hand of the Egyptians and to bring them up out of that land into a good and spacious land, a land flowing with milk and honey. (Exod. 3:7–8)

God called Moses to lead his people out of Egypt. Moses was reluctantly obedient, but Pharaoh didn't get the memo. Pharaoh refused to allow his slaves to leave—there were bricks to make, pyramids to build—so God sent a series of plagues. There were ten plagues in all, everything from darkness to frogs (*frogs? really?*)[1] to the death of the firstborn. Finally, Pharaoh relented. The Israelites looted their former masters and marched out, a million strong, toward the Promised Land.

They had not gotten far when God told them to turn around, backtrack, and camp by the Red Sea (Exod. 14:2).

Um, right by the water? Cutting off our escape route?

Yes, Moses—by the sea.

That's when Pharaoh decided that good slaves were too hard to find. He and his army set out to bring them home. The Israelites looked up to see the chariots bearing down on them. They turned around, and there was the Red Sea. Trapped.

Moses must have misunderstood. God would not lead them to a dead end, would he?

We do not know what to do, but our eyes are on you. (2 Chron. 20:12)

3

Not all pain is bad, and not all suffering is bad news. Sure, some things we go through are just rotten, and the only good is the good that can come out of it. An injury-causing automobile accident or a painful, fatal illness stinks, and no one is saying we should be happy for the mere fact that we are in pain (although we can be happy about the good that God can bring out of it—more about that later). There are some predicaments, though, that we whine and moan about when it is in fact the best thing that could have happened. And for even the worst thing we can imagine, we can't imagine how God can use it for our good or what he may have in store for us.

Take my job situation as an example. Look at it one way, and when our small firm called it quits, it was nothing more than a failed business, full of uncertainty and anxiety. I lost what I thought was an ideal situation, and I could not see at the time where God was leading me.

It took awhile. I spent a few years at another firm, a good firm, but the work was not what I wanted to do. Then there was the disappointment of unsuccessfully interviewing for a legal teaching position. All of this experience, though, and all of these contacts, worked together to put me in the right place at the right time. I'm now a constitutional lawyer in state government, and I've found what was missing professionally. The friendships I have made in my new office have been tremendous. And I've worked on issues such as defending child protection laws that, at the end of the day, make me feel like I've made a difference.

We ask *why do bad things happen to good people*, but we can't always tell whether the things that happen to us are good or bad. I thought it was a "bad thing" when our firm called it quits and when there were other bumps in the road. I see now that I was indeed where I was supposed to be, and had I not gone through those experiences, I would not have later gotten the job that I love so much.

---

*The unfolding of your words gives light;
it gives understanding to the simple. (Ps. 119:130)*

4

We are not very good at judging what is best. Our perspective is limited. We cannot see into the future like God can, and we do not have perfect understanding of the past like God does. We are "squinting in a fog, peering through a mist" (1 Cor. 13:12 *The Message*). We look at things through tunnel vision, focusing on the immediate present and how we feel *right now*. God, on the other hand, has a longer view and has more on his mind than our comfort.

So the job loss may be painful at the time, but it very well may be a bridge to a better situation. The relationship we want so desperately to work may not be for the best, and we aren't able to see it at the time. The heart attack may frighten you and get you off-track for a bit, but it could be what spurs you to start taking better care of yourself so that you will have more years of service. Is the job loss, the breakup, or the heart attack bad or good? It stinks when it happens, but in the end will you be better off for having gone through this storm? Before you decide, you really need the whole picture. The difficulty comes when God chooses not to give you the whole picture.

He does that a lot.

The psalmist describes God's Word as "a lamp for my feet, a light on my path" (Ps. 119:105). This is a picture of step-by-step guidance, not a once-for-all explanation of the entirety of God's plan. As the Israelites left Egypt, God guided them with a cloud by day and a pillar of fire by night, showing them one step at a time; he did not give them a map to Zion and leave them be.

He often deals with us the same way, giving us only what we need for that day and choosing, in his wisdom, not to show us the future. That includes not showing us how he will guide us through the weeks to come, the good he will bring out of suffering, and the person he will mold us into. And that makes it hard for mere mortals to know whether, in the long run, something that happens to us is "good" or "bad."

Just ask Joseph and Esther. They were hurting at the time of their trials, no doubt about that, but once they knew the whole story, they saw their circumstances in an entirely different light.

You intended to harm me,
but God intended it for good. (Gen. 50:20)

5

Joseph

Talk about your sibling rivalry.

Jacob (the grandson of Abraham) had twelve sons, but Joseph, the second youngest, was the apple of his eye. Jacob "loved Joseph more than any of his other sons," and gave Joseph the famous coat of many colors (Gen. 37:3). The other sons *hated* Joseph.

One day when the older brothers were out tending sheep and saw Joseph coming, they had the chance to shut him up once and for all. They first conspired to kill Joseph but decided instead to sell him into slavery (Gen. 37:12–36).

So Joseph became a slave in Egypt in the home of Potiphar, one of Pharaoh's officials. He could have curled up in a bitter ball and pouted for the rest of his life, but Joseph made the most of his circumstances. Everything he did, he did well, and Potiphar gave him more and more authority until Joseph was running the household (Gen. 39:1–6).

Potiphar was not the only one to notice Joseph. Mrs. Potiphar got an eyeful herself and liked what she saw. When Joseph refused her advances, she made false accusations against Joseph. Potiphar threw Joseph in prison where he sat unjustly for over two years (Gen. 39:7–20; 41:1).

Joseph gained a reputation in prison for being able to interpret dreams. When Pharaoh had a couple of strange ones, they brought Joseph out of the lockup. Joseph explained that the dreams revealed God's plans for Egypt: the land would have seven years of plenty, followed by seven years of severe famine. So . . . might be a good idea to start stocking up (Gen. 41:1–36). "Great idea," said Pharaoh, and he put Joseph in charge—not just of the food collections, but of all Egypt. Joseph became Pharaoh's second-in-command (Gen. 41:37–45).

Meanwhile, back in the Promised Land, Joseph's father and brothers were hungry. The famine affected them, too, and when Jacob heard there was food in Egypt, he sent his ten oldest remaining sons to buy food (Gen. 42:1–5). And guess who was minding the store.

It had been over twenty years, so the brothers did not recognize Joseph, but he recognized them. Joseph did not reveal himself at first—maybe he needed time to sort out his feelings—and sent them back to fetch the youngest brother Benjamin (or be called out as spies) (Gen. 42:7–16).

When they returned with Benjamin, Joseph came clean. He must have known what they would think and feel about facing a brother they had sold into slavery, so Joseph put it in perspective for them. Joseph saw the big picture, see, and did not hold a grudge against his brothers. That is because God used the entire situation to save their lives: "I am your brother Joseph, the one you sold into Egypt! And now, do not be distressed and do not be angry with yourselves for selling me here, because it was to save lives that God sent me ahead of you" (Gen. 45:4–5).

Later, when Jacob died, Joseph's brothers again feared retribution, but Joseph explained it all once more: "Don't be afraid. Am I in the place of God? You intended to harm me, but God intended it for good to accomplish what is now being done, the saving of many lives" (Gen. 50:19–20).

Maybe you had bad intentions, but God didn't, and he's in control.

So Joseph's family moved to Egypt, where there was food. They stayed and prospered, and their family, which became the Israelite nation, became so numerous that the Egyptians began to fear them. (This is how they came to be enslaved, four hundred years before Moses led them out of Egypt.)

Now, was being sold into slavery by your brothers and thrown into prison for no reason a bad thing? Of course it was. No doubt Joseph was sad, angry, lonely, and discouraged to be so rejected. But that's just part of the picture. God used those events to put Joseph in a position of prominence in Egypt. Because Joseph was where he was, when he was, God used him to take care of the family throughout the famine.

And that's a good thing.

WHY ME? (And Why That's the Wrong Question)

Who knows but that you have come to your royal position for such a time as this? (Esther 4:14)

6

Esther

You didn't say no to the king, not without greatly reducing your life expectancy. But when King Xerxes of Persia asked Queen Vashti to show off her beauty to his party guests, she thought she would rather not, thanks. The king's advisors were worried to death that wives everywhere would start standing up to their husbands, so they decided the king should fire Vashti and get a new wife (Esther 1:1–22).

To find the new queen, they gathered maidens from all over Persia. One of those maidens was Esther, a Jew. (This was the time when the Israelites were living in Babylonian exile.) Esther and the other maidens took beauty treatments for a full year and then reported to the king's chambers for a tryout (Esther 2:1–14).

Just imagine: a young teenage girl, orphaned, living in a foreign land, seized and forced to be a concubine. Would you blame Esther if she asked, "Why me?" Would you blame her if she wondered if God had forgotten all about her? Sure, Xerxes chose Esther for his queen (Esther 2:17), but for a faithful Jew, that is not the path Esther would have chosen. If God had a plan, it was probably hard for Esther to get behind it at this stage in the story.

As usual, though, there is more to the story. Before she was recruited for the royal job fair, Esther lived with her older cousin Mordecai. Mordecai was also a faithful Jew, and he refused to bow down to Haman, one of King Xerxes's aides. Haman liked that not at all, and he convinced Xerxes to sign an order that would eradicate the Jews a few months down the road (Esther 3:1–15). Xerxes, you see, had no idea that his new queen was an Israelite (Esther 2:20).

"Aha!" Mordecai thought. "Esther can convince the king to save us!" And he sent Esther word that she should go to the king and get him to fix things (Esther 4:1–8).

The trouble was, though, that no one—not even the queen—could go to the king uninvited. Unless the king pardoned the party-crasher, the punishment was death (Esther 4:9–11). Mordecai, however, was starting to see God's handiwork and sent a message to Esther:

> Do not think that because you are in the king's house you alone of all the Jews will escape. For if you remain silent at this time, relief and deliverance for the Jews will arise from another place, but you and your father's family will perish. And who knows but that you have come to royal position for such a time as this? (Esther 4:13–14).

Who knows but that you became queen for just this moment? Maybe your trial has a purpose, and this is it!

Esther decided that if God had placed her into those unpleasant circumstances so that she would be in position to act, then she would act. At the risk of her life, she went to the king, and Xerxes was compassionate to Esther and her people. He entered a second order permitting the Jews to defend themselves on the appointed day. Esther saved her people's lives. Or rather, God saved his people, through his servant Esther.

Would you say something "bad" had happened to you if you were yanked out of your living room and thrown into a dictator's bedchambers? Me, too. Esther might have agreed with us at first. Later, though, I bet she had a different point of view. Because Esther was where she was, when she was, God used her to save an entire nation.

And that's a good thing.

Jesus replied, "You do not realize now what I am doing, but later you will understand." (John 13:7)

7

I love my job, and I am so grateful for secure and rewarding work and the friends I have made. It makes me see my career path in a wholly different way. The path seemed rocky at the time, but I see now that it was carefully laid out.

One of the best parts of my career journey is the way it has helped my faith. If I lose my job tomorrow, I can look back on years of God's faithfulness. Maybe, perhaps, that can help me not lose heart. I hope that when a storm of any kind comes, I will remember how God has been at work and taken care of me even when I could not see it, and I will not doubt his guidance.

Maybe that is one of the reasons he did not fill me in on his entire plan. He was getting me to a particular place at a particular time, and he wanted me to learn to trust him along the way.

And maybe that is why God did not tell the Israelites why he wanted them to camp next to the Red Sea when Pharaoh's army was on the move. The people did not know what God had in store; they saw only the obstacle. Even though they had seen God's power demonstrated through the ten plagues, they doubted. They asked Moses, "Was it because there were no graves in Egypt that you brought us to the desert to die? . . . It would have been better for us to serve the Egyptians than to die in the desert!" (Exod. 14:11–12).

O ye of little faith. Of *course* God had an escape route planned. It happened to go through the middle of the Sea. God told Moses to raise his staff, and God parted the waters (Exod. 14:21–22). When the Egyptians followed, God released the waters, and the entire Egyptian army drowned (Exod. 14:26–28).

The Israelites would stray from God at times over their history, but immediately after the Red Sea miracle, their faith was strong:

> That day the LORD saved Israel from the hands of the Egyptians, and Israel saw the Egyptians lying dead on the shore. And

when the Israelites saw the mighty hand of the Lord displayed against the Egyptians, the people feared the Lord and put their trust in him and in Moses his servant. (Exod. 14:30–31)

The parting of the waters, and all the miraculous signs leading up to that miracle, was a crucial part of Israel's history. God was not only rescuing his children, he was also giving them a lesson in his faithfulness and power to help them through the rough times to come. He often reminded them, "But as for you, the Lord took you and brought you out of the iron-smelting furnace, out of Egypt, to be the people of his inheritance, as you now are" (Deut. 4:20). The entire process of moving from slaves to landowners was a sermon: *You can trust me. I love you. I keep my promises, and I have the power to take care of you. You can trust me.*

At the time that the Israelites were stuck between Pharaoh and the water, it looked like disaster, but only because they could not see that God would destroy Pharaoh's army. It looked like disaster, but only because they could not see that God was giving them a concrete example of his power and faithfulness that would strengthen them in the battles to come. Because the Israelite people were where they were, when they were, they had one less opposing army to contend with and witnessed a miracle that would, if they let it, cement their faith in God's power and goodness.

And that's a good thing.

For now we see through a glass, darkly; but then face to face: now I know in part; but then shall I know even as also I am known.
(1 Cor. 13:12 KJV)

8

When the crucifixion was imminent, Jesus was determined to be faithful to God's plan. That does not mean, however, that he looked forward to the pain. "My soul is overwhelmed with sorrow to the point of death," he told his sleepy disciples (Matt. 26:38). "Take this cup from me," he prayed. "Yet not what I will, but what you will" (Mark 14:36). His anguish was so great that the tiny capillaries near the surface of the skin burst, "and his sweat was like drops of blood falling to the ground" (Luke 22:44). Yet he went through the suffering. Willingly. He knew what it would accomplish.

If you asked Jesus whether the crucifixion was a good thing or a bad thing, what do you think he would say?

The next time you wonder why some awful thing has happened to you, remember Joseph. Remember Esther. Remember the Israelites and the Red Sea. Is it possible that you, or someone else, will be better off because of the storm you are going through? Is it possible that God is going to use this time to strengthen your faith? Is it possible that he has a plan to get you to the other side of the brick wall you have run up against, and you just can't see it yet? Is it possible that what looks bad now is in fact for the best?

When Joseph was sold into slavery by his brothers and thrown into prison for a crime he did not commit, Joseph had no idea a famine was coming. When Esther was marched to the headquarters of Harem, Inc., she had no way of knowing that her entire nation was going to receive a death sentence. And when the Israelites were backed up against the Red Sea, they had no way of knowing that the army bearing down upon them would not see the dawn.

What will you know at the end of your trial that you do not know now?

It may be that God knows something you don't, and what you think is a roadblock is really a bridge. It may be that God will use this trial to refine your character, to get you to a better place, to equip you for ministry, or to be a blessing to someone else. He may seek to glorify himself in the way you handle the trial, or he may be reaching out to someone else through your pain.

Whatever it is, if we just get past our bitterness and give him the wheel, something great is going to come out of the struggle.

And that's a good thing.

Notes

1. I have a sister who is terrified of frogs. This would have been one of her least-favorite plagues.

The Voyage of Life

One summer in college, I worked for a few weeks in Washington, DC. Every spare moment I toured monuments, museums, and government buildings. The National Gallery of Art was a favorite, and each visit I found myself lingering in a small, square room displaying *The Voyage of Life*, a series of four paintings by Thomas Cole.

Cole, a nineteenth-century American artist, depicts the voyager's journey along the river of life, beginning with childhood.[1] There, the voyager is an infant, guarded by an angel who steers the boat. The serene landscape symbolizes the sheltered life of childhood.

The second painting shows a youth who pays no attention to the angel. The youth has taken the tiller himself and looks ahead eagerly at what awaits him, anxious to take the world by storm. He does not even notice the rocks and rapids awaiting him downstream.

The third shows an adult man alone in the boat, the tiller now gone, lost in the rapids. Reality sets in and the voyager's confidence is gone. While the angel still watches over him, the voyager cannot see his protector and must rely on faith.

Finally, old age. The voyager has survived the trials of life and has made it to the end in a battered boat, the hourglass of time featured in the earlier paintings now gone. The guardian angel appears again and points the voyager, happy and at peace, toward the heavens where other angels wait to take him home.

At twenty, I stared at these paintings for hours on end, mainly at *Youth*. I related to the young man who believed himself to be in charge of his destiny with nothing but good things ahead. Like the youth in the painting, I don't think I even noticed the white water in the background. I had no concept that life would present trials as well as joy.

WHY ME? (And Why That's the Wrong Question)

Nearly a quarter-century after those first visits, we took our son to Washington, and I found myself again in the National Gallery. I had forgotten all about Cole's paintings until I rounded a corner and the memories flooded back. I stared, and stared some more, lost again in the journey.

This time, though, it was not the youth I related to. I was at a completely different stage of my own journey, and at forty-four, I found myself staring at the third painting, *Manhood*. Like Cole's voyager, I have realized that people cannot avoid all the rapids of life and that we do not always control our own fates. Like the voyager, I cannot always see my Protector, but I have learned to have faith that he is there.

If I live so long, I plan to go back in twenty-five more years. I have a feeling that a different painting in Cole's series will get most of my attention.

Notes

1. Images of the series are available on the National Gallery of Art's website:

   Childhood—www.nga.gov/fcgi-bin/timage_f?object=52450&image=12547&c
   Youth—www.nga.gov/fcgi-bin/timage_f?object=52451&image=12552&c
   Manhood—www.nga.gov/fcgi-bin/timage_f?object=52452&image=12558&c
   Old Age—www.nga.gov/fcgi-bin/timage_f?object=52453&image=12564&c

Chapter 6

DOES GOD CARE?
(Of Course He Does)

We may wonder if God cares about our suffering when it appears that he is not acting. The promises of the Bible and the actions of Jesus show that God indeed cares very much.

1

As evil as it is to kill another human being, mankind is nothing if not industrious, and we sometimes take murder to another level. When one group of people tries to wipe out another, we call it genocide.

Six million Jews in Nazi Germany. Millions of Hindus, Muslims, and Sikhs caught on the wrong side of a border during the 1947 partition of India. The Hutus and Tutsis each took a shot at the other in Burundi. About eight hundred thousand people in about a hundred days in Rwanda. Twenty thousand mass graves in the killing fields of Cambodia. Bosnia. Somalia. Who knows how many in Darfur?

While these examples are all in other countries, think about slavery and the Trail of Tears before you get too judgmental. And lest we start thinking that people have evolved past this sort of thing, remember that most of these events happened pretty recently in our history.

WHY ME? (And Why That's the Wrong Question)

> *Why do you always forget us?*
> *Why do you forsake us so long? (Lam. 5:20)*

It is hard enough to accept that humanity is so depraved that we can behave like this toward one another. It is harder still to understand how God can let this kind of thing go on. When there are wholesale executions of hundreds, thousands, *millions* of people on the insane basis of the color of their skin, or their ethnic heritage, or their religion, or whatever the trumped-up excuse . . . If that is not enough for God to intervene, then what on earth *would* be?

It's the kind of thing that makes people ask, "Does God care?"

> *Why, LORD, do you reject me and hide*
> *your face from me? (Ps. 88:14)*

2

Even the disciples, who walked and talked with Jesus and saw his miracles up close, wondered if God cared about them. The question crossed their minds as they paddled for their lives, and Jesus slept in the back of the boat.

After a day of healing and teaching by a lake, Jesus and his disciples were sailing to the other side for some peace and quiet (Mark 4:35–36). Exhausted, Jesus slept, even when "a furious squall came up, and the waves broke over the boat, so that it was nearly swamped" (Mark 4:37).

And the disciples said, "No worries—Jesus is with us! Nothing can happen to us if God is in the boat."

No, they didn't (and neither would we). They were scared. They struggled with oars, bailed water, and cut occasional glances over their shoulder at a certain napping itinerant preacher.

We don't know if they expected a miracle, or if they just wanted Jesus to grab a bucket, but they finally gathered the courage to wake him up. And someone (I'm guessing Peter) said, "Teacher, don't you care if we drown?" (Mark 4:38).

Does God care?

I say to God my Rock, "Why have you forgotten me? Why must I go about mourning, oppressed by the enemy?" (Ps. 42:9)

3

At the risk of spoiling the suspense, I'll give you the end of this chapter now. Yes, God cares. He cares about the suffering of the world, and he cares about your suffering specifically. He knows exactly what is troubling you and it concerns him very much.

Yet in our anguish, we sometimes feel abandoned. We assume that if God cared about our suffering, he would stop it. So when God does not answer our prayer immediately, in the precise way that we want, we doubt and ask God if he even cares that we're drowning, that we're sick, that we're lonely, that our house is under water, that we still don't have a job, or that she's seeing someone else.

The rain is still falling. The wind is still blowing. The waves are breaking over the boat and we're *sinking*, dang it. God hasn't fixed the problem in a way that our five senses can detect, so we think it must be that he doesn't care about us at all.

Teacher, don't you care?

Yes, God cares. He *told* us so, and he *showed* us so.

Why do you hold back your hand, your right hand? (Ps. 74:11)

4

God cared about Hagar, a little-known Egyptian woman from ancient times. She had no importance as the world measures such things, but she was important to God.

Pregnant and unmarried is not the best time to quit your job, but Hagar had reached her limit. Her mistress, Sarah, who was married to the father of Hagar's unborn child, made Hagar's life a living hell and Hagar ran (Gen. 16:6).

It all started when God promised an old man that he would have a child. God told Abraham that he would make him into a "great nation" (Gen. 12:2). God promised, "I will make your offspring like the dust of the earth" (Gen. 13:16), and "a son who is your own flesh and blood will be your heir" (Gen. 15:4b).

But Abraham was old. And Sarah was old, well past the normal childbearing years. After ten years of waiting, they made the mistake so many of us do—they stopped waiting on the promises of God and did things their own way.

Trouble ensued.

Sarah said to Abraham, "The LORD has kept me from having children. Go, sleep with my slave; perhaps I can build a family through her" (Gen. 16:2). So Abraham slept with Hagar, and Hagar got pregnant.

Maybe Hagar resented being a womb for rent. Maybe she grew attached to the baby growing inside her and did not want to give him up. For whatever reason, she began to "despise" Sarah (Gen. 16:4). Sarah returned the sentiment, and Hagar fled into the desert.

As an Egyptian, Hagar had no apparent place in the new race God was creating through Abraham, and we do not know what she believed about God at this point in the story. We can safely assume, though, that she was discouraged. She felt abandoned. She was alone in a desert with nowhere to go, with no way to support her child. Would you blame her if she felt forsaken?

God did not blame Hagar for crying out in anguish, and he did not ignore her cries. Hagar was not "nothing" to God; she was his daughter. He sent an angel to her and told her that she should name her son Ishmael, which means "God hears," because "the Lord has heard of your misery" (Gen. 16:11). God reassured her that Hagar and Ishmael would not be forgotten, and their descendents will be "too numerous to count" (Gen. 16:10).

Why would God do that? Why would he take personal interest in an Egyptian woman and take the time just to make her feel better? He certainly did not have to, but he did, because he cared. God cared about Hagar's suffering, and he told her so. By including the story in the Bible, he tells us so, too. He is "the Father of compassion and the God of all comfort" (2 Cor. 1:3).

> *The eyes of the Lord are on the righteous,*
> *and his ears are attentive to their cry. (Ps. 34:15)*

5

God—the limitless, eternal creator—is beyond our understanding. We know of him only what he chooses to reveal. He reveals his character to us in the Bible, and one of the things he must really want us to understand is that "God is love" (1 John 4:8). With love, the Father created you, "inside and out," and knows everything about you: "You know me inside and out, you know every bone in my body; You know exactly how I was made, bit by bit, how I was sculpted from nothing into something" (Ps. 139:15 *The Message*). He put every cell in place, just as he wanted, out of nothing. He even knows how many hairs are on your head (Matt. 10:30). *Of course* God cares. He tells us so over and over.

Isaiah says God feels his people's sorrow, and "in all their distress he too was distressed" (63:9). God does not simply observe our pain; he hurts right along with us. The psalmist tells us that "as a father has compassion on his children, so the LORD has compassion on those who fear him" (Ps. 103:13). Peter asks you to "cast all your anxiety on him because he cares for you" (1 Pet. 5:7). Nahum tells us, "He cares for those who trust in him" (1:7). And Jesus tells us that we can lean on him: "Come to me, all you who are weary and burdened, and I will give you rest" (Matt. 11:28).

Think how you feel when someone you love is suffering (if you have children, think of them). Where do you think that compassion comes from? We are created in God's image (Gen. 1:27). Anything good in us—our ability to reason, to love, to feel empathy, to be generous, even our sense of humor—comes from God. Any good in us is a small, and very incomplete, picture of who he is.

We are fallen and imperfect, of course. We do not love perfectly the way God does, and we do not have perfect compassion the way he does. However, if we can feel compassion at all, we can be confident that God does, too—to infinity. The heartbreak we feel when our children hurt themselves, and the way we would do anything for them (so long as it is in their best interest), is nothing compared to the compassion God feels when he aches with us.

While it should be enough that he tells us he cares, he did not stop there. He came to live among us and *showed* us that he cares.

It is the Father, living in me,
who is doing his work. (John 14:10)

6

God's glory is so magnificent that no one can look on him and live (Exod. 33:20). If we cannot see God, how can he show us that he cares? By becoming a man, living among us, and letting us watch what he does.

Jesus, the Son, is one with God the Father (John 10:30). In fact, Jesus said that "anyone who has seen me has seen the Father" (John 14:9). "God was pleased to have all his fullness dwell in him" (Col. 1:19). Therefore, when we look at what Jesus said and did, we see the very character of God.

What did Jesus do during his three-year ministry? Well, he did not give people cancer. He didn't break up marriages, create a credit crisis, or cause any person harm in any way. Quite the opposite: Jesus made things better everywhere he went.

Take blindness. There was no law against discrimination against persons with disabilities in biblical times, and a blind person had few opportunities outside of begging. Jesus did not close people's eyes; he *opened* them (John 9; Mark 8:22–26; Mark 10:46–52).

Take leprosy. That disease was a big deal in the first century. Lepers were cast out of the community, so they had to deal with loneliness and rejection on top of the physical pain and deterioration. Jesus did not give people leprosy; he *cured* them (Matt. 8:1–3; Luke 17:11–19).

He healed the invalid (John 5:1–9), the paralyzed (Mark 2:1–12), the deformed (Mark 3:1–5), the hemorrhaging (Mark 5:25–34), and the deaf and mute (Mark 7:31–35). And when Jesus went to a funeral, it stopped being a funeral: sorrow turned into a celebration when the widow's son, Jairus's daughter, and Lazarus were raised from the dead (Luke 7:11–17; Luke 8:40–56; John 11:38–44).

Are these the actions of a God who does not care?

Jesus felt the pain of each person who came to him. In one crowd, Jesus healed all the sick who were present "to fulfill what was spoken through the prophet Isaiah: 'He took up our infirmities and bore our diseases'" (Matt. 8:17).

Even the *way* he healed showed compassion, such as when he "looked up to heaven . . . with a deep sigh" over a deaf and mute man's suffering (Mark 7:34). He wept at the pain caused by Lazarus's death (John 11:35). Nobody touched a contagious leper, but Jesus was willing to give a leper the simple gift of human contact before healing: "Filled with compassion, Jesus reached out his hand and touched the man" (Mark 1:41 NIV 1984). *Filled with compassion,* the Bible says:

- "When he saw the crowds, he had compassion on them, because they were harassed and helpless, like sheep without a shepherd" (Matt. 9:36).
- "When Jesus landed and saw a large crowd, he had compassion on them and healed their sick" (Matt. 14:14).
- "I have compassion for these people" (Matt. 15:32).
- "As he approached Jerusalem and saw the city, he wept over it" (Luke 19:41).

He helped everywhere he went. He provided for a wedding banquet (John 2:1–11). He reached out to outcasts (Matt. 9:10–11; Luke 19:1–9; John 4:1–15). He fed the hungry (Mark 6:30–44; 8:1–9). His question was "What do you want me to do for you?" (Matt. 20:32). His message was "go in peace and be freed from your suffering" (Mark 5:34b). "Take heart" (Matt. 9:22). "Don't cry" (Luke 7:13). "Do not let your hearts be troubled" (John 14:1). "In me you may have peace" (John 16:33).

And then he carried his own cross to the top of a rugged hill, took a place among common criminals, and gave you his life.

This is a God who cares.

Why, LORD, do you stand far off?
Why do you hide yourself in times of trouble? (Ps. 10:1)

7

Do not forget that as a man, Jesus had his own burdens and faced his own pain and hardship. He could have stayed in heaven, but he chose freely to live with us and walk in our shoes, to feel what we feel.

Because he suffered the same things we suffer, he understands what we go through. If you and I have never been homeless, we might have compassion for a homeless person, but we still have no real understanding of her trials. Jesus, though, went through it all. That is great news, because we can take our problems to him boldly:

> For we do not have a high priest who is unable to empathize with our weaknesses, but we have one who has been tempted in every way, just as we are—yet he did not sin. Let us then approach God's throne of grace with confidence, so that we may receive mercy and find grace to help us in our time of need. (Heb. 4:15–16)

When you are overwhelmed, think of Jesus in the Garden of Gethsemane, sweating drops of blood and saying, "My soul is overwhelmed with sorrow to the point of death" (Matt. 26:38). Take your sorrow to him.

When you feel abandoned, think of Jesus on the cross saying, "My God, my God, why have you forsaken me?" (Mark 15:34). Take your desperation, and your questions, to him.

When you are sad, lonely, discouraged, or anxious, take it to Jesus. He felt every pain that we feel. How could he *not* care?

Record my misery; list my tears on your scroll—
are they not in your record? (Ps. 56:8)

8

The Psalms are a great read when you are at the end of your rope. The psalmists ask the human questions and raise the human doubts, but they come back to faith and confidence in God's love. Tracing their feelings from point A to point B can take you on the same journey.

"I cried out to God for help; I cried out to God to hear me," one psalmist wrote (Ps. 77:1). He wondered, "Will the Lord reject forever? Will he never show his favor again? . . . Has God forgotten to be merciful? Has he in anger withheld his compassion?" (Ps. 77:7, 9). How many times have you felt that way?

Then the writer does something we all should do when it seems like God has forgotten us: he takes a moment to remember all of God's care in the past, which gives him hope for the future. "Once again I'll go over what GOD has done, lay out on the table the ancient wonders; I'll ponder all the things you've accomplished, and give a long, loving look at your acts" (Ps. 77:11–12 *The Message*).

That's what we should do when we wonder if God cares. Think on what the Bible tells us about God's compassion. Remember all Jesus did that shows us how much he cares. Remember what he has done for you personally, from the cross two thousand years ago to the strength he provided last week. Say to God, "My soul is downcast within me; therefore I will remember you" (Ps. 42:6a).

Why, my soul, are you downcast? Why so disturbed within me? Put your hope in God, for I will yet praise him, my Savior and my God.
(Ps. 42:11)

9

Dr. Paul Brand treated lepers in India in the mid-twentieth century. He saw pain, and he saw people who may have wondered if God cares. To the question "Where is God when it hurts?" Dr. Brand famously replied, "He is in you, the one hurting, not in it, the thing that hurts."[1]

I don't know why genocides happen. I don't know why people are so cruel, or why God does not stop it. Of all the possible answers, though, God-not-caring is off the table. The Bible leaves no room for that conclusion.

We still may wonder sometimes, when the waves pound us. We might ask, with the disciples, if God cares if we drown. For the disciples, Jesus calmed the literal storm: he simply said a word, and the wind and waves came to an abrupt halt (Mark 4:39). For us, he may only calm the storm in our heart, giving us strength to overcome our fears.

Either way, he is in the boat with us. Either way, God cares.

I have heard your prayer and seen your tears;
I will heal you. (2 Kings 20:5)

Notes

1. Philip Yancey, *Disappointment with God: Three Questions No One Asks Aloud* (Grand Rapids: Zondervan, 1992), 183.

Chapter 7

WHY DOESN'T GOD DO SOMETHING?
(He Has, He Is, and He Will)

We ask, "Why doesn't God *do* something about our suffering?" We forget, though, all that God accomplished on the cross to solve the problem of sin and evil, what he is doing already in the present, and all he's promised for our future.

1

Hurricane Katrina did not seem especially significant as it passed the Bahamas and southern Florida, but it gained strength over the Gulf of Mexico and quickly grew to a Category 5 monster. It lost strength, then grew again, before its second landfall in Louisiana.

The storm surge led to fifty-three levee breaches in and around New Orleans, flooding about 80 percent of the city. Water rose to rooftops in some areas, up to fifteen feet in others. More than seven hundred bodies were recovered in New Orleans—some several weeks after the storm—but the inability to identify many bodies leaves the death count in controversy.

WHY ME? (And Why That's the Wrong Question)

Many survivors left the city. A quarter of the population did not come back.

Why do you hold back your hand, your right hand? (Ps. 74:11)

New Orleans was not the only area affected by the hurricane, not even close. But hitting a major metropolitan area, particularly one so ill-suited to withstand a storm surge, multiplied the damage.

Why? A nudge here, a nudge there, and the death count would have been cut by more than half. Hundreds of thousands of survivors would not have had their lives uprooted. God could have stopped it, but he didn't. He "who shut up the sea behind doors" (Job 38:8) could have kept it there, but he didn't.

We see the pictures of devastation, the crowds huddled inside the Superdome, the ocean pouring through the city streets, and we ask, "Why doesn't God *do* something?"

Awake, Lord! Why do you sleep? Rouse yourself! (Ps. 44:23)

2

Cleopas wondered the same thing. He lived near Jerusalem at the time of the crucifixion. Rome conquered Judah a century past, and Cleopas and his countrymen had lived under an iron fist ever since. They dreamed of the day when centurions were not walking the streets, when Israel would be free again.

Then Jesus appeared on the scene. His signs and wonders probably gave Cleopas hope that Jesus was the Messiah, the one who would "rescue Israel." That must mean, Cleopas thought, that they would be rid of the Romans once for all. Hopes were especially high as the Passover approached and Jesus entered the city under triumphant shouts of

"Hosanna! Hosanna!" from the multitudes who had traveled to the city for the annual celebration (John 12:13).

But messiahs don't die, right? When Jesus died an ugly, common death on Friday, Cleopas thought his dream was over. He stuck around town for the Sabbath (no walking allowed). Then Sunday morning, after some crazy talk from a group of women about an empty tomb, Cleopas and a friend began the seven-mile hike to Emmaus. Heads down, feet dragging, they walked and talked about what might have been.

Arise, Lord! Lift up your hand, O God.
Do not forget the helpless. (Ps. 10:12)

A stranger stepped up beside them somewhere along the way and walked with them. He asked, "What are you guys talking about?"

Cleopas and his pal looked at the man in astonishment. *What do you think we're talking about? Have you been under a rock? Are you the only person in Jerusalem who doesn't know what happened to Jesus?*

"He was a prophet, powerful in word and deed before God and all the people. The chief priests and our rulers handed him over to be sentenced to death, and they crucified him; but we had hoped that he was the one who was going to redeem Israel" (Luke 24:19–21).

But we had hoped. Such sad words. Cleopas thought God was going to *do* something.

How long, Sovereign Lord, holy and true, until you judge the
inhabitants of the earth and avenge our blood? (Rev. 6:10)

3

We established last chapter that God cares, which is great. It's better than him *not* caring, obviously. Somebody caring, however, will not rebuild a flooded city. Caring by itself, with no action to back it up, will not get rid of the Roman conquerors. Compassion alone does not fix things, and we want God to *act*, to end the injustice, to stop the war, to cure the disease. A little less conversation and a little more action, if you don't mind.

That's all Cleopas wanted. He wanted God to intervene the way he had for Israel in the past. You can't blame Cleopas for wanting those things, but he had completely missed the point. He wanted God to redeem Israel, and God *did* redeem Israel. The redemption was not in the expected form of a political revolution but something much better: the price of our sins was paid and we were reconciled to God. The crucifixion was not the death of a dream but the means by which God offers salvation. God *had* done something. Cleopas just missed it.

Often, we miss it, too. We want God to do something, but we fail to realize that God *has* done something for us in the past (the cross), that he *is doing* something for us in the present (the provision of the Holy Spirit, his presence, and the intercession of Christ), and he *will do* something for us in the future (hello, heaven!).

Oh, that you would burst from the heavens and come down!
(Isa. 64:1 NLT)

4

Much of what we really wish God would do, he has already done. The end of our story was written two thousand years ago on the cross.

Without the cross we are all dead in the water, dead in our sin. Our sin separates us from God. If we get stuck in a place of willful rebellion, God will leave us alone, hiding "his face from [us], so that he will not hear" (Isa. 59:2). We all sin, as we established in an earlier chapter, and "the wages of sin is death" (Rom. 6:23). And there is nothing we can do about it. Left to our own devices, there is exactly zero chance of escaping an eternity of separation from God.

Our eternity is more important than anything that can happen in the few short decades we spend in this life. No matter how much suffering takes place now, it is far more critical to settle where we will be once that suffering ends. Yet even if we understand this, human beings cannot, on their own power, remove themselves from the penalty of sin.

So God gave us a way: he sent his son to save us (John 3:17). He came to do what we could not, "for the Son of Man came to seek and to save the lost" (Luke 19:10). He did it "to bring you to God" (1 Pet. 3:18).

How was this accomplished? By Jesus taking our punishment upon himself. "He himself bore our sins in his body on the cross, so that we might die to sins and live for righteousness; by his wounds you have been healed" (1 Pet. 2:24). He was killed because of *our* sin, beaten because of *our* wrongs, and wounded so that *we* can be healed (Isa. 53:5).

What does this mean? Only everything. Because of the cross, our sins are taken away (Heb. 9:28). Guilt does not have to weigh us down. The past is past, our record is not held against us, and our sin is as far removed "as the east is from the west" (Ps. 103:12).

Resolving past sin is great, but what about today's sin? That's covered, too. Because of the cross, God can help us be less sinful and more like him. Because of the cross, we are rescued "from the present evil age" (Gal. 1:4). Because of the cross, we are no longer slaves to selfish sin. We no longer live for ourselves, but for God (2 Cor. 5:15). The cross gives us freedom *not* to sin, and we have a new heart and a new spirit within us (Ezek. 36:26).

If God is already tugging at you, he may be giving you an inkling of how far you have to go—how far we *all* have to go. You know your sins are forgiven, but you want more. You want abundant life. You want your behavior to match the part of your heart that loves God and is grateful for his grace. The cross is the answer, for only through Jesus' death and resurrection does our road to sanctification begin. And because he is alive, he lives *in* you during your trial.

Yes, you may still need surgery. Your husband may or may not come back. The hurricane may not change course, and the levees still may fail. But when it comes to the biggest problem people face—our sin—God already *has* done something. Even if we or someone we love dies a physical death, we have infinite time in infinite goodness ahead.

He saw that there was no one, he was appalled that there was no one to intervene; so his own arm achieved salvation for him, and his own righteousness sustained him. (Isa. 59:16)

5

The cross is in the past, but God's activity in our lives was not a one-time event. He remains active in our present. He sent his Spirit to teach and guide us, Christ intercedes for us in the throne room of heaven, and he is present with us at all times.

In the last hours before his crucifixion, Jesus keyed in on a few especially important issues for his disciples. Soon he would not be with them in the body. The disciples were scared and confused when Jesus told them about his coming death, so he comforted them with some great news. He was sending help: "And I will ask the Father, and he will give you another advocate to help you and be with you forever—the Spirit of truth" (John 14:16–17). Jesus was sending the Holy Spirit, the third person in the Trinity. The disciples would never be alone or without help.

Neither will we.

Worried about remembering all the sermons you heard from Jesus, Peter? "But the Advocate, the Holy Spirit, whom the Father will send in my name, will teach you all things and will remind you of everything I have said to you" (John 14:26).

And you, James—afraid you won't know what to say when you go out to preach? "The Holy Spirit will teach you at that time what you should say" (Luke 12:12).

Hey, Andrew—nervous about getting confused about what it all means? "But when he, the Spirit of truth, comes, he will guide you into all the truth. He will not speak on his own; he will speak only what he hears, and he will tell you what is yet to come" (John 16:13).

Jesus would send them out soon to tell the world of his death and resurrection, but he was not going to send them out alone. The Spirit would be with them every step of the way, reminding them of Jesus' teaching, helping them understand, always testifying to the truth.

The same Spirit lives in us, too, if we are saved (1 Cor. 3:16). That's one of the ways we know that we *are* saved (1 John 4:13). He teaches us just like he taught the disciples and molds our characters (Gal. 5:22–23), always working to make us more like Jesus (1 Pet. 1:2).

Whether you turn to the right or to the left, your ears will hear a voice behind you, saying, "This is the way; walk in it."(Isa. 30:21)

6

God the Son is also at work for us in the present through the ministry of intercession. Isaiah says Jesus "bore the sin of many, and made intercession for the transgressors" (53:12). Paul says that now that Jesus died, was raised again, and ascended into heaven, he "is at the right hand of God and is also interceding for us" (Rom. 8:34). He "is able to save completely those who come to God through him, because he always lives to intercede for them" (Heb. 7:25).

Somehow, God the Son is appealing for us before God the Father. For *you*. Pleading for you earnestly. For *me*. I have never found a definitive explanation for what it is exactly that Jesus is doing when he intercedes, but I picture him saying, "It's okay—he's with me. Jim may not look like much, but he's one of mine."

While I may not understand it completely, I do know that there is no one I would rather have as my advocate. And right this moment, as you endure whatever trial you are facing, the creator of the universe is in *your* corner, with you on his mind, your name on his lips.

God *is* doing something.

> *So we may boldly say: "The Lord is my helper; I will not fear. What can man do to me?" (Heb. 13:6 NKJV)*

7

And for the future? That's when it will all come together.

Think of that situation where you were wronged, and it was so hard to bear because (it seemed to you) the wrongdoer faced no consequences for his sin. He got away with it, and you were left holding the bag. It's the *injustice* that is grating whenever we see the powerful squash the weak with impunity.

I have no idea if Casey Anthony, accused of killing her daughter, committed a crime. I have no idea if O. J. Simpson murdered his wife. In both cases, the public *believed* there was a miscarriage of justice. There was an uproar when people thought someone got away with it.

There is always an uproar when we think someone got away with it. They will *not* get away with it, not in the long run.

The day will come when all wrongs will be made right. Those who follow Christ will have their tears wiped away and will never die, never face sorrow or loneliness, and never know pain, in a home Jesus prepares (John 14:1–3).

And that person who in this life faced no consequences for his wrongs? "The wicked will not go unpunished" (Prov. 11:21). He *will* get his comeuppance in eternity, unless . . . unless he too places his faith in Christ.

One way or the other, every sin will be punished, either through punishment of the person who committed the sin, or, if they believe, through the punishment that Jesus took for us on the cross. One way or the other, there will be justice for every wrong ever done, to any person, from the beginning of time to the end.

I know, I know: you would like to see more *contemporary* justice, where no one gets away with it, even for a little while. Remember, though, that if God handed out instant justice, it would apply to us, too. I won't presume to speak for you, but I would have died about twenty-seven times in the last five minutes if God punished all sin instantly. Thank goodness for his mercy, where he says, "For my own name's sake I delay my wrath; for the sake of my praise I hold it back from you, so as not to destroy you completely" (Isa. 48:9).

In the meanwhile, though, we will see other people appear to profit from their sin, to "get away with it." And sometimes we will get away with it, too, in the short run. But the day will come when God will have his justice.

Why doesn't God do something?

He will. You better believe it.

Do not fret because of those who are evil or be envious of those who do wrong; for like the grass they will soon wither, like green plants they will soon die away. (Ps. 37:1–2)

8

It takes faith to wait on God when we see injustice and know that only in his time, in his way, will it be made right. Habakkuk had to learn that lesson, too.

WHY ME? (And Why That's the Wrong Question)

Habakkuk asked God why he wouldn't just do something about all the injustice in Israel: "How long, LORD, must I call for help, but you do not listen? Or cry out to you, 'Violence!' but you do not save? . . . Why do you tolerate wrongdoing?" (Hab. 1:2–3).

God answers and tells Habakkuk that he ain't gonna believe what God has in store:

> Look at the nations and watch—and be utterly amazed. For I am going to do something in your days that you would not believe, even if you were told. I am raising up the Babylonians, that ruthless and impetuous people, who sweep across the whole earth to seize dwellings not their own. (Hab. 1:5–6)

God was not going to let the Israelites get away with anything, and he loved them too much to let them stay in rebellion. He would send the Babylonians to take the Israelites into exile until they decided to pay attention to God again.

Habakkuk did not like God's answer at all. The Babylonians weren't nice guys, and Habakkuk did not understand how God could use an evil people to do holy work. God couldn't use evil to achieve a righteous purpose, Habakkuk thought, so God would just have to change his plans. God answered this concern as well. Sort of. "And the LORD answered me: 'Write the vision; make it plain on tablets, so he may run who reads it'" (Hab. 2:2 ESV). *I'm going to tell you about the Babylonians, and I want you to write it down in such simple terms that anyone could understand it at a glance as they run by the billboard.*

"For still the vision awaits its appointed time; it hastens to the end—it will not lie. If it seems slow, wait for it; it will surely come; it will not delay" (Hab. 2:3 ESV). *The thing is, it won't happen right away. But I said it, and it shall be. Just wait.*

"Behold, his soul is puffed up; it is not upright within him, but the righteous shall live by his faith" (Hab. 2:4 ESV). *The Babylonians will get* theirs. *All people who trust in themselves will get theirs. You have to have faith. You have to trust in me.*

Justice would come—to the wicked in Israel and in Babylon and everywhere in the world—but it would come in God's time. We have to trust in him. God *will* do something. He said so.

> He will swallow up death forever. The Sovereign LORD will wipe away the tears from all faces; he will remove his people's disgrace from all the earth. The LORD has spoken. (Isa. 25:8)

9

Did Cleopas learn that lesson? His walk started out in defeat but ended in victory.

Remember the stranger walking with Cleopas and his friend? He was the resurrected Jesus, who chose not to be recognized at first. Jesus used the Scriptures to help them understand that it was necessary for the Messiah to suffer and that suffering did not mean failure.

> He said to them, "How foolish you are, and how slow to believe all that the prophets have spoken! Did not the Messiah have to suffer these things and then enter his glory?" And beginning with Moses and all the Prophets, he explained to them what was said in all the Scriptures concerning himself. (Luke 24:25–27)

How would you like to have heard that Bible study? Jesus may have referred to Isaiah's discussion of the suffering servant (Isa. 53). He may have discussed the Passover (Exod. 11–12), the serpent that was lifted up in the desert to give life (Num. 21), or the Levitical sacrifices. Whatever Scripture he used, Jesus explained that his ministry was indeed salvation, but not the kind of salvation that Cleopas and his friend were hoping for. It was salvation that could be purchased only by death: "Very truly I tell you, unless a kernel of wheat falls to the ground and dies, it remains only a single seed. But if it dies, it produces many seeds" (John 12:24).

And Cleopas learned that the whole time he had been complaining about God not doing something, God was working his fingers to the bone on his behalf.

So do not fear, for I am with you; do not be dismayed, for I am your God. I will strengthen you and help you; I will uphold you with my righteous right hand. (Isa. 41:10)

10

The ministries of the cross, of the Holy Spirit, and of intercession and the coming glories of heaven apply to all believers. They are God's past, present, and future actions on behalf of all his people.

Certainly, though, God is also doing something in individual lives. As horrific as Hurricane Katrina was, there were plenty of signs that God was at work.

He was at work in protecting a group of six children who had been separated from their parents in the evacuation. A six-year-old was found wandering at an evacuation point, carrying a five-month-old and surrounded by toddlers, guarding the brood until rescue workers located their parents at another evacuation site.[1]

God was doing something in the life of Courtney Miles, a young man growing up virtually on his own, as he commandeered a bus and drove as many as he could to safety.[2] Relocated to Oakland, California, Miles finds his life turned around and counts the hurricane as a blessing.

God was doing something through the American Red Cross, which deployed seventy-four thousand volunteers in the first two weeks, provided millions of meals, and provided shelter to 160,000 evacuees. He was doing something when Feeding America collected over thirty-three million pounds of food for Katrina relief, when over thirty thousand United Methodist volunteers helped muck out homes and rebuild, and when people across the region opened up more than forty-five thousand beds to perfect strangers.

Sure, people wrote the checks and gathered the cans and did all those things, but you will never convince me that God was not behind it all. David may have held the sling that killed Goliath, but God was working through David. Moses may have raised his staff, but God parted the waters. Likewise, people may have helped with recovery from Katrina's damage, but it was God working through people. It was God doing something.[3]

---

*The LORD is my strength and my shield;
my heart trusts in him, and he helps me. (Ps. 28:7)*

11

What about your life? Does it feel like God has forgotten you? Are you still waiting on him to do something?

If it seems like God is doing nothing, remember his provision on the cross, the indwelling of the Holy Spirit, and the promise of heaven to come.

And more than that, remember that God may be doing something in your life at this moment, although it may be different from what *you* think is best. It may not be the miracle that you would rank as first choice, but if he is sending other people to love you through the pain, or even simply giving you the strength to get through the trial, God is at work.

Our God is not a God of lounge chairs and mai tais. He is a God with sleeves rolled up. We may not always recognize his work, because what we think he should be doing is not always for the best, but he is at work.

God *is* doing something.

Notes

1. Ellen Barry, "A Child in Charge of '6 Babies,'" *Los Angeles Times*, September 6, 2005, www.chicagotribune.com/news/nationworld/chi-0509060168sep06,0,3659601.story.

2. Lisa Hix, "Katrina as a Blessing: It Sent One Teen Here," *SFGate.com*, August 27, 2006, http://articles.sfgate.com/2006-08-27/opinion/17308554_1_bus-hurricane-katrina-neighbors.

3. When I first heard that the New Orleans levees failed, I was leaving Children's Hospital in Birmingham, where the edge of the storm was passing through. I had just finished sitting with my son as he slept postsurgery. (See Chapter 11 for details.) Ironically, I had been listening to Led Zeppelin's "When the Levee Breaks" on my iPod.

Chapter 8

WHERE'S MY MIRACLE?
(It May Be Better Than You Dared Hope)

> We may wonder why God does not heal us physically the way he healed so many in the Bible. Divine healings still happen, but the biblical miracles were not a promise to heal *everyone*. Sometimes God performs miracles in our spirits that we cannot see but that are even more wonderful than a physical healing.

1

He went seeking a miracle.

Paralyzed, the man could not get to Jesus on his own, but he had friends willing to carry him. He would soon find that his disability was not the only barrier between him and Jesus.

Months before that day, Jesus created a stir in Capernaum when he healed a demon-possessed man and Peter's mother-in-law (Mark 1:21–31). The "whole town gathered at the door" to be healed (Mark 1:33). So when Jesus came back to Capernaum after a preaching tour of Galilee, it was standing room only. The man and his friends could not get near the door. Four of them carried their pal up to the roof, made a hole in the mud and straw, and lowered him down to Jesus (Mark 2:1–4).

So what did Jesus do? Was he angry at being interrupted mid-parable, chunks of mud falling on his head? Not at all. That is exactly the kind of faith and determination that God loves. God says many times that if we seek him with all our hearts, we *will* find him (Deut. 4:29; Prov. 8:17; Jer. 29:13; Matt. 7:7).

Jesus looked at the man with compassion and said, "Son, your sins are forgiven" (Mark 2:5).

What? "Now wait just a minute," the still-paralyzed man may have thought. "I came here to you, carried like a sack of potatoes, my legs withered and still beneath me, and you *forgive my sins*? Do you really think that's why I'm here? Well, that's just great. Let me get up and thank you—oh wait, *I can't.*"

The man had heard the stories about all the healings Jesus had done (or he wouldn't be there), and it wouldn't surprise me at all if he felt a little left out.

"Where's *my* miracle?" he may have thought.

Then He took the child by the hand, and said to her, "Talitha, cumi," which is translated, "Little girl, I say to you, arise."
(Mark 5:41 NKJV)

2

He went seeking a miracle.

Jairus was living every parent's nightmare. He fell at Jesus' feet (always a good place to start) and said, "My little daughter lies at the point of death. Come and lay Your hands on her, that she may be healed, and she will live" (Mark 5:23 NKJV).

Jesus followed Jairus to his home, but the neighbors said it was too late. The little girl was dead.

"No," Jesus said, "she's only sleeping."

And then he said, "'Talitha, cumi,' which is translated, 'Little girl, I say to you, arise'" (Mark 5:41 NKJV).

And she did.

As a kid, I loved finding that story in the Bible and seeing Grandma's name. She was named for that story: Talitha Cumi Collins.[1] It is a unique name, to say the least, and she was a unique woman, but she was a typical grandma in the way she loved family get-togethers.

One of those get-togethers was a wedding, and my cousin Amy was there. Amy and I are close in age and were inseparable playmates as kids. It was my first chance to meet her daughter Caroline, an absolute angel with her mom's blonde hair, blue eyes, and playfulness.

Amy said she had always dreamed of having two little girls. She was delighted to share that she was expecting her second, another daughter.

Later in the day, Caroline started to run a slight fever. Amy, her husband Rod, and Caroline went home to Chattanooga the next day, and the fever didn't seem to be getting better.

It was meningitis.

Two days after the wedding, little Caroline died.

No one said, "*Talitha, cumi.*"

Where was Caroline's miracle?

I will give you hidden treasures, riches stored in secret places,
so that you may know that I am the LORD, the God of Israel,
who summons you by name. (Isa. 45:3)

3

In the last two chapters, we have seen that God cares deeply about our suffering—he loves us, after all—and he is active in our past, present, and future. And we all know the stories from Sunday school about the parted waters, loaves and fishes, and even emptied tombs. God can do what he wants, and we are confident of his power. We also know that at least on some occasions, God wants to perform miracles. Many people came to Jesus with a problem and walked away without it.

So why raise Jairus's daughter and not Caroline? Why are there blind people today when Jesus opened so many eyes two thousand years ago? Why do people still starve to death when Jesus could feed a multitude with one little boy's lunch? Why are there so many examples from the Bible where God poked his finger into the world and rearranged nature for one person's benefit, and yet this problem, or this sickness, is still in my life? Is there something wrong with me? Where's *my* miracle?

If we are not careful, it is easy to read the biblical miracles as a promise, some sort of an invitation to get in line because this is the way God is going to treat everybody. That cannot be so, though, because God does *not* heal everybody. What then do the miracles mean?

It seems that Jesus' three-year ministry—when he walked among us physically—was a time unique in the way God interacted with mankind. If you look at the way the miracles were treated by the Gospel writers, Jesus was doing more than healing and feeding. He was giving us signs of his deity and showing us, in a visible way, what he longs to do within our hearts.

I have no doubt that miracles still happen, and sometimes they are in the form of physical healing. Often, though, the miracles of today are things we cannot see, but a spiritual miracle is no less dear than a physical miracle. While we might think we would rather God fix our legs, it really is just as spectacular, or even more so, when he fixes our broken hearts.

That doesn't stop us from wanting a physical miracle, of course. And absolutely we should pray for physical miracles, for ourselves and for others. If God chooses not to answer that prayer in the way we want, though, it does not mean that he is being grinchy. We may feel disappointment at such times, but we should also have faith that God loves us and knows what is best. Perhaps we can accept his sovereign will more graciously when we understand the purposes of the biblical miracles.

Perhaps we can better accept not getting the miracle we want when we understand that God often intervenes in a way that is even *better*.

Believe me when I say that I am in the Father and the Father is in me; or at least believe on the evidence of the works themselves.
(John 14:11)

4

If Jesus' miracles do not represent a promise that God will fix all our earthly problems, what do they represent? They had many purposes, it seems to me, and one of them was to show us that Jesus came from God.

Even the people closest to Jesus had questions about who he was. His cousin, John the Baptist, may have played with Jesus as a child, but he still had questions.

John had more reason than most to figure out who the Messiah was, because his entire purpose in life was to help prepare the world to receive him (Mark 1:2–4). Could it be Jesus? There must have been talk, a look in Cousin Mary's eye, a *difference* about Jesus that got John wondering. Then John baptized his cousin and saw the heavens open above them, saw a dove descend from the skies and land on Jesus, and heard a voice from heaven, booming, "This is my Son, whom I love; with him I am well pleased" (Matt. 3:16–17).

Well, that ought to do it, right? Shouldn't that convince John the Baptist that Jesus was a little out of the ordinary? It appeared so when John pointed to Jesus and said, "Look! The Lamb of God!" (John 1:36). And yet he still wanted to hear it from Jesus' mouth, so one day he sent a couple of his followers to ask Jesus point-blank: *Is it you?* "Are you the one who is to come, or should we expect someone else?" (Luke 7:19).

Jesus sent his cousin a message: "Go back and report to John what you have seen and heard: The blind receive sight, the lame walk, those who have leprosy are cleansed, the deaf hear, the dead are raised, and the good news is proclaimed to the poor" (Luke 7:22). According to Jesus, John could identify the Messiah by looking at Jesus' miracles.

John knew his Scriptures, and these words would have meant something to him. He may have pulled out his scrolls and checked Isaiah's prophesies about the Messiah:

- "Then will the eyes of the blind be opened and the ears of the deaf unstopped. Then will the lame leap like a deer, and the mute tongue shout for joy" (Isa. 35:5–6).
- "But your dead will live, LORD; their bodies will rise" (Isa. 26:19).
- "The LORD has anointed me to proclaim good news to the poor" (Isa. 61:1).

See, John would have known that Jesus' miracles were *signs* that the Old Testament prophecies were fulfilled in Jesus.

Others would know the same. When a group of Jews asked him if he was the Messiah, Jesus said, "The works I do in my Father's name testify about me" (John 10:25). And the disciple John (a different John) emphasized seven miraculous signs to show that Jesus was God's Son.

Disciple John's purpose for writing his Gospel was that we "may believe that Jesus is the Messiah, the Son of God, and that by believing you may have life in his name" (John 20:31). The miracles were part of John's proof. When Jesus turned water into wine at a wedding, the disciple said it was "the first of the signs through which he revealed his glory" (John 2:11). Healing a royal official's son was the second (John 4:54). Jesus healed a man by a pool in Bethesda (John 5:1–15), fed the five thousand (John 6:1–13), walked on water (John 6:15–21), healed a blind man (John 9), and raised his friend Lazarus from the dead (John 11). Seven signs in all, specific miracles that said, "This is my son."

This, then, was at least one purpose of Jesus' miracles, to give us assurance that Jesus was who he said he was. And who did he say he was? No less than God himself.

Asked at his trial if he was "the Christ, the Son of the Blessed One," Jesus said, "I am" (Mark 14:61–62). "Yes, it is as you say" (Matt. 26:64 NIV 1984). "You are right in saying I am" (Luke 22:70 NIV 1984).

When a Samaritan woman mentioned the Christ, Jesus told her, "I who speak to you am he" (John 4:26 ESV).

On other occasions, Jesus referred back to God's conversation with Moses from the burning bush. When Moses asked God his name, God said, "I AM" (Exod. 3:14). Thus, if you called yourself "I AM," you were saying, "I'm God"—a good way to get stoned in those days. Jesus used that name when he told a group of religious leaders, "Before Abraham was born, I am!" (John 8:58). The hypocrites understood exactly what Jesus was claiming and started looking around for rocks (John 8:59).

Then when Jesus was arrested in the Garden of Gethsemane, he asked the soldiers, "Who is it you want?" When the soldiers said, "Jesus of Nazareth," Jesus replied, "*I am* he" (John 18:5; italics added). There was so much power in Jesus' claim that the soldiers "drew back and fell to the ground" (John 18:6). Jesus' claim literally knocked people off their feet.

"I am the bread of life," he said (John 6:35).
"I am the true vine" (John 15:1).
"I am the good shepherd" (John 10:11).
"I am the light of the world" (John 8:12).
"I am the gate" (John 10:9).
"I am the way and the truth and the life" (John 14:6).
"I am the resurrection and the life" (John 11:25).

So make no mistake about it—Jesus claimed that he was the Messiah. He claimed that he was the Son of God. He claimed that he *was* God. That would be absurd and blasphemous coming from anyone else, so God gives us the miracles (eyewitness accounts recorded in the Bible) as proof. After all, no ordinary man could do the things Jesus did. Only someone with God's favor, someone sent by God himself, could bring back the dead. God would not empower a charlatan to do such wondrous things, so we can look at the miracles and know that Jesus was neither crazy nor a liar when he made his outrageous claims.

The miracles were not a message from God that anyone can come to him and get anything he or she wants. God was not saying that sickness and death and disability would be wiped out (not yet, anyway). He was saying, "This is my Son, whom I love."

> *I am the bread of life. Whoever comes to me will never go hungry, and whoever believes in me will never be thirsty. (John 6:35)*

5

I believe that another purpose of the miracles was to show us what God can do for us on the inside. They were living parables, sermons in action. Put on your English-major hats, search for the symbolism in the miracles, and get a picture of the unseen work God does in our spirits.

Water into Wine

On one hand, turning water into wine did nothing more than save a wedding host from the embarrassment of running out of refreshments. Look deeper, though, and consider that water—a necessity of life—is often a *symbol* of life. God provided life-giving water to the Israelites in the desert (Exod. 17:5–7), and Jesus referred to himself as the source of living water (John 4:13–14). Wine, though, is a symbol of *abundant* life—joyous and celebratory life. Jesus did not just turn water into wine; he showed us that he takes the ordinary and makes it special.

This is what he wants to do for us, to take the dull, the bland, and the droll and turn it into something exceptional. He does it every day, turning despair into hope, loneliness into contentment, fear into peace, and sinners into saints. It's why he came.

Leprosy

When Jesus healed lepers, he changed their entire lives, not just their health (Luke 5:12–16; 17:11–19). The disease ate away at the body, but it also separated a person socially. No one wanted to be near a contagious leper, so he was a lonely outcast.

A healing of leprosy is a picture of how God frees us from sin. Just as leprosy permeates and decays the body, sin engulfs us and eats away at our spirits. Just as the disease separates the leper from society, sin separates us from God. When God forgives our sin, our spirits are healed, and we are restored to God's presence. Forgiveness of sin is even more life-changing and restorative than being an ex-leper.

And the Blind Will See

Jesus opened the eyes of many blind men (Matt. 20:29–34; Mark 8:22–25; Luke 18:35–43; John 9:1–41). One minute Bartimaeus saw nothing, but after an encounter with Jesus, the world was in living color. No more stumbling around, no more waiting for someone to guide him to his begging spot. But what of the nimrods who tried to shush Bartimaeus up, to keep him from "bothering" Jesus? (Luke 18:39). Sure, they could see physically, but they were *spiritually* blind and unable to understand why Jesus came or for whom he came.

Another beggar received his sight in the ninth chapter of John's Gospel. On the Sabbath, no less, which was a no-no in the eyes of the self-righteous Pharisees. When they protested, Jesus said, "For judgment I have come into this world, so that the blind will see and those who see will become blind" (John 9:39). The Pharisees scoffed and asked, "What? Are we blind too?" (John 9:40).

Were they ever.

And so are we. Like a litter of puppies born with eyes closed, we come into this world blinded by sin. We cannot see our need for a savior. We cannot see that sin is even a problem or that Jesus has the only cure. We are so blind that we don't even *know* that we are blind. But God says, "Woe to those who are wise in their own eyes, [a]nd prudent in their own sight!" (Isa. 5:21 NKJV). And just as Jesus healed physical blindness in the Gospels, he opens our spiritual sight and lets us see the truth of our sinful condition and his grace.

Loaves and Fishes

One day when a crowd approached Jesus, he asked his disciples, "Where shall we buy bread for these people to eat?" (John 6:5).

The disciples looked at the five thousand hungry people and must have thought Jesus was out of his mind. They didn't have money to buy that kind of food. All they had was some poor kid's lunch—five loaves and two fishes—and the kid's mom probably had not intended to pack for the whole bunch. But Jesus took that tiny amount, gave thanks, and started passing it out.

And he kept passing it out.

And he passed it out some more, until every single person had enough to eat.

The miracle shows Jesus' compassion, sure, for he does indeed care about everyday physical needs like hunger. But Jesus also made a larger point. When the crowd kept following him asking for more miracles and more food, Jesus explained that he does much more than meet physical needs. Just as food is sustenance that we need to live physically, Jesus is nourishment for our spirit: "I am the bread of life," he said. "Whoever comes to me will never go hungry, and whoever believes in me will never be thirsty" (John 6:35). And, "I am the bread of life. Your ancestors ate the manna in the wilderness, yet they died. But here is bread that comes down from heaven, which anyone may eat and not die" (John 6:48–50).

The grumbling in your stomach is not your most pressing need. You can eat a meal and take care of your physical hunger, but in no time you will be hungry again. For that longing deep in your soul, though—that spiritual hunger—there is a person who can meet that need once and for all. By divinely feeding a crowd with physical bread, Jesus showed us he is the Bread of Life.

Lazarus, Come Out!

And then there was Lazarus. He and his sisters, Mary and Martha, were friends of Jesus. Word came to Jesus that Lazarus was deathly ill, and Jesus said, "This sickness will not end in death. No, it is for God's glory so that God's Son may be glorified through it" (John 11:4).

Maybe the sickness did not *end* in death, but it sure stopped off along the way. Jesus took his time getting to Bethany, and by the time he arrived, Lazarus had been in the tomb for four days.

Jesus was not surprised by Lazarus's death, and he surely knew what he had planned, but that did not keep his heart from breaking when he saw the grief of Lazarus's friends and family. "Jesus wept" (John 11:35). This was not the world as he created it, but a world broken by our sin, and he longed to make it right. After telling Martha that he is "the resurrection and the life" (John 11:25), Jesus called in a loud voice, "Lazarus, come out!" (John 11:43).

And Lazarus did.

Do we really need to walk through the lessons here? Take your pick. We start out as walking corpses, dead in our sin. We can no more save ourselves from sin than we can open our coffins and climb out of the grave. Only the grace of God can save us and make us live again spiritually, and by raising Lazarus, Jesus showed us that he can do exactly that.

Or you can see in this miracle that Jesus was pointing the way to his own resurrection and all that the resurrection purchased for us. How can the grave hold him when he can call his friends forth?

Or this miracle can assure you that God's promises of a future home in heaven are not empty promises. When he says that in the last day the dead in Christ will rise, we know he can do it. He did it for Lazarus; he will do it for you.

By raising Lazarus, though, Jesus was not saying that no one else will die. By healing many, Jesus was not saying that sickness was a thing of the past. That is not the promise of the miracles. The promise of the miracles is that he *can* do these things and that he is the Son of God. The promise of the miracles is that he stands ready and willing and able to fix our hearts and spirits just the way he fixed the bodies of Bartimaeus, Lazarus, and so many others.

But if I do them, even though you do not believe me,
believe the works, that you may know and understand that the
Father is in me, and I in the Father. (John 10:38)

6

Is it any less a miracle if Jesus heals our spiritual blindness and not our physical problems? If he forgives our sin, but does not heal our legs? What is a miracle, after all, except God doing the impossible? And that is true whether it is a visible miracle or one that takes place within our spirits.

Let's revisit the lame man with his four friends from the beginning of this chapter. He would have said that paralysis was his biggest problem, but God knew better. When the man asked for one thing—that which was the most obvious problem in his own mind, and we can't blame him for that—Jesus gave him something that was even better and cured his sin problem. And make no mistake, forgiveness was indeed the better gift, because the man would be lame only for this life, but eternity awaits.

Still, I don't think we should blame the man if a little disappointment flickered across his eyes when he thought he would be carried away from his meeting with Jesus. We are equally likely to be disappointed when God chooses not to give us physical healing. And we, too, sometimes get confused about what our biggest problem is.

If we are sick, or if a loved one is sick, that to us is our biggest problem. When the levee is breaking, our prayer is that God will do something about the floods. But God may know that even in the face of immediate danger, our big problem is really selfishness, or impatience, or the ridiculous notion that we don't even need God.

Of course, we should never assume that God refuses to heal us, or anyone else, because we have been bad; rather, the point is that our holiness is a greater priority to God than our health. He may or may not intervene with your body, your job, or your relationship, or whatever it is that is most on your mind right now, but whatever that is may not really be your biggest problem. And if you pay attention, you will see God at work, even if it is not to give you your first choice of interventions.

There are miracles all around us, and we miss them every day. It truly is a miracle—something only God can do—when an illness leads someone to faith in Christ. It is a miracle when our satisfaction in him soothes the sting of a broken marriage. It is a miracle when he gives us peace and calms our fears. It is a miracle sometimes when we just make it through the day without falling apart, because it is his grace—his divine intervention—that props us up.

Before you pout and say, "Where's *my* miracle?" make sure you didn't miss it. Maybe God did something miraculous that you couldn't see but that is even better than what you asked for. Maybe you asked him to fix your legs, but he forgave your sin instead, and that is no less miraculous or wondrous than the parting of the Red Sea.

I pray that out of his glorious riches he may strengthen you with power through his Spirit in your inner being. (Eph. 3:16)

7

We've left the poor lame man on his mat long enough, longer even than Jesus did.

It would have been enough for the man to leave lame but restored to God's fellowship. Yet Jesus chose to heal his body as well, and the man "walked out in full view of them all" (Mark 2:12). And in this case, Jesus even told us why he was doing it. No one could simply look at the man after Jesus forgave his sins and see that anything had really happened, so Jesus performed a physical miracle to back up his authority. He healed the man's legs so you may "know that the Son of Man has authority on earth to forgive sins" (Mark 2:10).

I don't know why my cousin's daughter died. The wrongness of it—caskets just aren't supposed to come in that size—made me as angry as I was sad at the funeral. I was not the only one with that reaction, but there were two people throughout the whole ordeal who were at peace: Rod and Amy, Caroline's parents.

Of course they were heartbroken and missed Caroline terribly, but they never questioned God, at least not where anyone could see it. They witnessed throughout the visitation and funeral, and Rod even spoke at the service. Asked how in the world they could be so calm, how they could speak of God's goodness at the very time they faced such grief, how they could be so strong and ruin the perfectly good fit the rest of us were ready to throw, Amy replied simply, "Grace. It's all grace."

No, God did not heal Caroline, but he gave Rod and Amy a miracle. He did the impossible and helped them get through it in a way that made them stronger than ever before. He held them in his arms throughout the hospitalization. He wept with them as they said goodbye. He propped them up and empowered them to show God's love in their time of greatest need. He gave them assurance that he would hold Caroline until they joined her, and Amy now has *three* little girls, one of whom is in heaven. Two are with her now, and they point to Caroline's picture and say, "That's Momma's other baby, and she loves her *soooo* much."

> *But he said to me, "My grace is sufficient for you,
> for my power is made perfect in weakness." (2 Cor. 12:9)*

We get all worked up about our comfort and about our physical world. We give bodily health a greater priority than our spiritual health, and we spend more time worrying about our happiness and financial security than about our character.

God doesn't. Our holiness and eternal security are more important to him, and they should be to us. So if he does not give you the miracle you want, that does not mean God isn't acting. It may be a miracle that you cannot see. And it may just be a greater miracle than you asked for.

Notes

1. My other grandmother was named Ethel Mae. If we had been blessed with a little girl, I think we would have had to look beyond my grandmothers for names.

MIKE & MIKE (2)

When we left Mike and Mike, the Reeds were getting great news from their doctor, and the Worleys had just learned of Mike's multiple myeloma. Things look up for Mike and April Reed, and while Mike and Pam Worley are just getting started, they at least have the comfort of a medical plan and an idea of what is to come.

How will they handle things when the news does not stay good and when plans give way to uncontrollable events? When each medical option presents another set of risks? When life doesn't stop just because you have cancer?

These are the times when a family learns to appreciate their relationship with God like never before. The cancer that can take life can also make them start truly living. The very disease that has the potential to make them fearful has the potential to make them stronger.

Strength is good. The Reeds and Worleys will need it as they continue to fight.

Reed

Tuesday, May 31, 2011, 3:17 PM (April)
Mike has relapsed. The PET scan showed that the cancer is back around his liver and spleen. We are unsure of the next plan.

Wednesday, June 1, 2011, 8:48 AM (Mike R.)
Yesterday was tough. I wanted so bad for my doctor to say that I was still in remission and to go home and give my wife and son a hug, but obviously that didn't happen. In sitting there with the doctor and

watch him do a "fumbleroosky" on the words to say because neither option is a good one, you start to think about what you truly believe.

. . . I began to start thinking of how mad at God I was going to be if this didn't turn out good and what I was going to say to Him on the car ride home. But, when the doctor told me the news, it was like I already knew it and I had an incredible calm about everything. I called April and she was the same way.

I'll tell you what I do know, though. I know that I don't put my hope in doctors. . . . Jesus said in John 16:33, "In this life you will have trouble, but take heart, I have overcome the world." No one ever said life was going to be easy. In fact, Jesus said that you WOULD have trouble. April and I don't have perfect lives, nor should we expect to. . . . So, what do we put our hope in? We put it in the Lord.

Worley

Monday, June 20, 2011, 7:15 PM (Mike W.)

First the big TV quit working, then my lap top died . . . and yesterday the dryer broke. You would think if you have something as bad as cancer you'd a least get a "break" from everything breaking!!! Ahhh, but life goes on as usual. . .

If we wake up in the morning breathing, we have a choice. We can choose to face our trials, give thanks and press on, or we can choose to give in to those trials and be consumed by them. Because life doesn't stop or cut you some slack, just because you have cancer (or anything else).

Reed

Wednesday, June 22, 2011, 11:16 AM (Mike R.)

April and I met with Dr. M today to discuss the biopsy results. The lymphoma is not in my bone marrow. However, my bone marrow scan showed myelodysplastic syndrome (MDS), a result of all the chemotherapy I have had over the years. MDS often develops into leukemia. . . .

Dr. M has spent lots of time researching and came up with three options:

1) Do nothing (this is the first time we've ever heard this).
2) Take a drug that COULD help both the MDS and Hodgkin's but could possibly be fatal, causing bleeding or other problems due to low counts.
3) Take a drug that would only help the MDS, which I have had before.

Obviously, none of these sound great. . . .

Thursday, July 7, 2011, 9:58 PM (Mike R.)

To be completely honest, things have been a little down for us lately. We found a study that says the survival rate for Hodgkin's patients with MDS is around 4 months. I don't say that for a huge pity party, but to be completely transparent in how we are doing. We have never really believed in statistics. After all, I had a 90-something percent chance of licking this in the first 6 months of treatment. However, this has gotten us a little down, frustrated and mad at God (which by the way is okay), and just wondering when will it be over.

I know where some of you will go with this . . . why do people like us have to deal with this and people like Casey Anthony go free? Well, let me first say that I am no better than her. My heart is evil and I am no more worthy of grace than she is, but it is what it is. We can't let anger take control of our lives.

Medically, we are almost out of options. All the more reason to fervently pray. I don't know why God has brought back this cancer and allowed the MDS. However, I do know that He loves April and

I more than we love each other and even ourselves. Maybe it is to exhaust all our options and ultimately heal me and show His glory and to show all of us that we need to look to Him for our answers and put our hope in Him. I just don't know.

. . . So, we fear the unknown of what is to come, but are going to take it one day at a time and pray for a miracle.

Worley

Monday, July 25, 2011, 5:16 PM (Pam)

Bring on Tuesday, because I've had about enough of Monday!!! Mike and I started out our day this morning headed to his treatment appointment at CCI at 7:50. At 7:48, they called and said not to come. There is a nationwide shortage of the drug Doxil (used in chemotherapy) and they had none to give him. . . .

Were we disappointed? Yes. Were we a little discouraged? Yes. Did we want to cry? Yes. Did I want to head to the nearest Krispy Kreme and drown my sorrows in a dozen hot ones? Yes. And all that is ok. We are all going to have disappointments and discouragements in our life. But how long will we wallow in it? I'll just be honest, sometimes I really, really like to get down in there and wallow around in my self pity and "woe is me" feelings! But as I was thinking about how I was going to handle all this news today, the funniest thing came to my mind. When I was a kid, there used to be this toy that stood about 2-3 feet tall and was a punching bag with the face of Bozo the clown. It was filled with air and had some kind of weight in the bottom of it to keep it standing upright. When you punched it, it would wobble to the floor and then bounce right back up with that goofy looking grin on its face. No matter how hard you hit it or how many times, it ALWAYS popped up, smiling right back at you. As I was thinking about that silly toy, I prayed, "God, let me be like that Bozo. No matter how hard I get hit during this journey and no matter how many times, let me get back up. Smiling."

Reed

Tuesday, July 12, 2011, 4:27 PM (Mike R.)

Yesterday was tough for me. I asked (the doctor) what we should do and she broke out into, "If there is a trip that you have been wanting to take for a while, take it. You need to go home and spend as much time with your son and wife as possible, and there are good hospice programs out there."

Man, when she said that, it was almost like my future, or lack thereof, flashed through my life with Trent, and I just lost it. I can't remember the last time I cried like that. It has been years. The thought of never seeing his first day of school, first home run, graduation, married, being baptized all flashed through me in about 10 seconds.

Then once the flames settled, I realized it was a spiritual attack. I was fearing the future. The Bible says, "God has not given us a Spirit of fear, but of power, love and sound mind."

. . . We are just begging and pleading for your faithful prayers. I don't know if any of you have ever been told that you are basically about to die and asked if you have a will ready, but that will get you in action mode pretty quick, brother. We won't give up.

Worley

Tuesday, August 16, 2011, 5:52 PM (Pam)

One minute we would be pumped up and full of faith and the next minute we were just down-right scared. But through it all, I've seen God work in a mighty way this week! I don't wish our problems on any of you, but I do wish you could see what I get to see, feel, and experience. It's like God in high-def! . . . I think that has been one of the blessings this cancer has brought me. I think it's making me a little more aware of each moment, because that is where I'm forced to live. . . . Maybe in that way, I can find something in cancer to be thankful for. Time ticks by, moment by moment, and before we know it days, weeks, even years have gone by without us really noticing or living. What if I chose to live each moment full—full of love, full of life, full of God's grace? Isn't that where life really is, in each moment? Those quick moments that make lasting memories, that change lives, that give someone else hope. That's where I'm striving to live, and thank you Mr. Cancer for helping me find my way there! You thought you would make things worse for me but God, my Great Big God, is turning it around and into something He can use in me. For that, I am thankful.

Reed

Monday, September 19, 2011, 11:21 AM (Mike R.)

I was hoping to give great news, but the cards fall where they may. My blood counts fell back down. . . . We don't know what the MDS is doing without a bone marrow biopsy, so tomorrow I am going to have one. . . .

This is a frustrating part of treatment because there is no definitive right answer to this problem. Dr. M is trying to do his best to treat me without killing me at the same time, but where is the line drawn? I have to admit that I have been frustrated too. I KNOW that God's Word says that because of his stripes, I am healed. I am just at the point of saying to God, "Okay, God, it's been long enough. There are enough lives who have been touched. I'll take the healing now please and get on with my life. Can't you use somebody else now?"

Thursday, September 29, 2011, 8:38 AM (Mike R.)
We still are trusting God with all this because it is a situation where it could get bad quick, but we just have to take it one day at a time and trust Him.

Worley

Tuesday, November 1, 2011, 11:25 AM (Pam)
Friday was the BIG day, day zero—transplant day. . . .

There is this peace, this amazing peace, that we all four feel. We don't head into this week worried or fearful, just peaceful. It is that peace from God that surpasses all comprehension and guards our hearts and minds (Phil. 4:7, look it up). It's the peace that people have been praying for God to fill us with, and He has been faithful to do so. I can't tell you how many texts and emails we received on Friday, all praying the same thing for us—peace and comfort. Each prayer meant so much to us, but can I just say, when you are receiving texts from your kids' friends, teenagers, who tell you they have been praying all morning for you, well, that's just about the best thing ever! That kind of makes me want to cry just thinking about it! Now, I don't fool myself into thinking this week (or the next couple) will be easy, but I know that this is the only way to walk through them! Me on my knees praying, my friends praying, and my kids' friends praying, that's how we will all four get through it! You just can't get any better than that!

Ah. So remission can give way to relapse. The fine plans of the expert medical staff give way to drug shortages. But the Worleys and the Reeds are anchored deep. They have a foundation of faith in the Rock, in a God who is bigger than their setbacks. They are honest about the times when they are discouraged, both to themselves and to God (which requires its own kind of bravery), but they still have hope.

Thus, Mike Reed can look at things realistically and acknowledge that no one has a perfect life, but he can put his hope in a perfect God. Medicine offers no more options—in fact, the chemotherapy that had seemed promising contributed to the MDS and complicated the situation—but God offers everything. He still believes in the power of prayer and still believes in the power of God to sustain him however those prayers are answered.

My hat is off to the Reeds. They are facing cancer like soldiers of Christ. That doesn't mean that they are completely free of fear or anxiety or frustration. They're human, after all. Rather, it means that they are not letting any of those feelings damage their faith. Bad news doesn't make them turn away from God; it makes them cling harder to the Rock.

With their own deep anchor points, the Worleys can press on even as they continue to deal with everyday struggles on top of the unique pressures of serious illness, and even when their treatment plan falls by the wayside. Of course, any plan involving chemotherapy is something other than first choice, but they at least, for a time, had the comfort of thinking they knew what was ahead. Then the TV breaks just like it does for people who do not have cancer, and then their chemotherapy drug is not available, but the Worleys do not fall. They do not give in to the temptation of despair, but get back up. Smiling. God is always front and center, God in "high-def," a view that comes more easily when circumstances force them to rely more on God.

Then again, neither family has had their last knock. You read of their struggles and their strength and know these families could be excused for asking, "Why me?" Perhaps, though, as the Worleys and the Reeds created their CaringBridge journals, they saw that nearly four hundred thousand other families had done the same, and they remembered they were not the only ones going through a trial. Perhaps any time they were tempted to wonder if God cares, that was the time they received a call from a supportive friend. And if they were tempted to wonder why such a thing would happen to "good" families like theirs, they remembered, as Mike Reed did, that everyone is in need of grace.

So now what? Both families are headed to a crisis point as they wait to learn the results of the MDS treatment (the Reeds) and the stem-cell transplant (the Worleys). Of course they are both praying for healing, but because they are asking the right questions, they also have confidence that God will work all things for good no matter the outcome.

They still, it goes without saying, have a very strong preference for what that outcome will be. As they should.

… PART THREE

The Right Questions

Chapter 9

HOW CAN THIS TRIAL DRAW ME CLOSER TO GOD?

> God calls us to draw near, but in our sin and stubbornness, we too often are content to drift away. We may not even hear God's call when life is smooth, but he can use suffering to pull us closer.

1

They say few trials are as emotionally intense as infidelity.

> *"I wanted to die, and I think death would have been easier than his rejection."*

> *"You could have told me I had a month to live, and I don't think it would have shaken me as much."*

Men and women I know who have experienced the trial of infidelity speak of a total loss of self-worth, a sense that some irreparable flaw of their own caused their spouse to stray.

> *"I felt like I was no man at all. Totally emasculated."*

> *"What was so wrong with me? Was I not pretty enough? Not loving enough?"*

> *"How stupid can I be to have missed all the signs? What an idiot. It's no wonder she cheated."*

They speak of a sense that the rug has been pulled out from under them. They can't be sure that anything is as it seems.

> *"Years of memories I can't trust anymore. I look at a photo from that time and realize he may have been thinking of someone else at that very moment. It was all a lie."*
>
> *"What was real and what wasn't? What is real now and what isn't?"*

Little wonder that a person betrayed finds it difficult to trust.

> *"It's not just that I don't know how to trust her; I don't know how to trust anybody."*
>
> *"What can I count on when the one person I thought had my back put a knife in it?"*

Little wonder that the future looks bleak.

> *"Can I ever love again? Can I ever be loved again?"*

What would such a trial do to a person's relationship with God? If you think the pain might make them feel distant from God, you would be right.

> *"Where was God? Is this what faithfulness brings?"*

But then again, if you thought it would drive them closer into the arms of Christ, you would also be right.

> *"It was when I felt like no one else on earth loved me that God's love began to feel real."*

Infidelity, like other trials, can lead a person away from God, but it can also drive a person nearer. It's up to us. If a person allows it, the very pain that makes him want to curl up and hide for the rest of his life can connect him to Christ like never before.

There is a place of quiet rest, near to the heart of God.[1]

2

If infidelity is so painful, would anyone enter into a marriage knowing that the other party will cheat? Ask Hosea.

Hosea!

"God? Is that you?"

I am. I want you to be my spokesperson in Israel to speak out against my people following false gods.

"I'm your man! What do you want me to do?"

A lot. But first, you will marry.

"Marry? That's fantastic! I've been lonely, and it would be great having someone to share my life. Is she . . . (I hate to ask this) . . . is she pretty?"

Of course. She is my creation. She is beautiful.

"Will we have children?"

Yes, three, and I will name them for you.

"Will I love her?"

Oh, yes. You will love her so much that it hurts.

"Will her love for me be true?"

That? Not so much. "Go and marry a promiscuous wife and have children of promiscuity, for the land is committing blatant acts of promiscuity by abandoning the Lord" (Hosea 1:2 HCSB).

So Hosea married Gomer. Just as God said, they had three children: a son named Jezreel, or "Scattered," because God would soon scatter the Israelites in exile at the hands of the Assyrians; a daughter named "No Compassion"; and a son named "Not My People" (Hosea 1:4–8 HCSB).[2]

And just as God said, Gomer cheated. She ran off after other lovers and left Hosea with the kids. Knowing it was coming did not make it hurt any less. It still pained Hosea to be on the receiving end of the jokes and put-downs as Gomer left one lover after another and finally resorted to prostitution. It must have crushed him to explain to No Compassion why Mom wasn't tucking her in tonight.

It hurt so much because Hosea loved Gomer. He was devastated and heartbroken. We have clues, based on the way Hosea phrased his prophesies, that he may even have secretly provided for Gomer while she was living with other men: "She does not recognize that it is I who gave her the grain, the new wine, and the oil" (Hosea 2:8a HCSB).

Why would God put his prophet through such agony? To make an important point. Hosea's life, his marriage, and his funny-named children were a sermon. God's loving people, his bride, had drifted away, deserting their God. They were cheating on him, prostituting themselves by following false gods (Hosea 4:10). They were adulterers, literally and spiritually, observing scandalous fertility rites. And Hosea's pain shows us how God hurts when we turn away.

God longed for the Israelites to draw near. He had tried in various ways to pull them back, through kindness and warnings, but the people continued in their rebellion. God had another arrow in his quiver, though. He would draw his people back through their suffering, and Hosea's life tells that story.

We read the story of Hosea, and we think how awful it must have been to be him. We put ourselves in Hosea's shoes and wonder how he must have felt when his wife humiliated and abandoned him, or how we would have responded in his place.

We miss the point when we do that. See, we are not Hosea in this story. We're Gomer.

We are not the loving husband sitting at home licking his wounds. We're the hooker.

The LORD is near to all who call on him,
to all who call on him in truth. (Ps. 145:18)

3

God repeatedly invites us to "draw near with a true heart in full assurance of faith" (Heb. 10:22 HCSB). "Draw near to God, and He will draw near to you," promises James (4:8 HCSB). The reason God created us is so that we might seek him and find him (Acts 17:27).

God clearly does not mean that we must go to a particular *place* to be near him. We are not closer to him in church or on a mountaintop. We cannot climb to God, because God is already everywhere. "Where can I go to escape Your Spirit? Where can I flee from Your presence? If I go up to heaven, You are there; if I make my bed in Sheol, You are there. If I live at the eastern horizon or settle at the western limits, even there Your hand will lead me" (Ps. 139:7–10 HCSB).

The "nearness" God desires of us is *relational*. Jesus likens it to the way branches are connected to a vine, us living in him and he living in us (John 15:1–17). With that nearness, we have joy and fruitfulness; without it, we can do nothing (John 15:5, 11). It is a daily, moment-by-moment dependence on God's love and a joy in his presence. So why do we not always feel that closeness?

There is an old joke about an elderly couple driving behind teenage sweethearts out on a date. The older woman notices how the girl is riding pressed up against her beau on the old-fashioned bench seat. She asks her husband from the passenger's seat, "Remember when we used to ride like that?" The old man responds, "Look who moved."

If we feel distant from God, it is because *we* pulled away. God has not revealed himself in the Bible to be fickle. He does not show himself as here one moment and gone the next. He is steadfast in his love. The picture he gives us is of one who stands and knocks (Rev. 3:20), a shepherd who goes out to search for one lost sheep (Luke 15:3–7), a woman who searches the entire house for one lost coin (Luke 15:8–10), or a father who stands on the porch gazing out to the horizon waiting for his lost son to return (Luke 15:11–31). He calls *all* the thirsty and poor to come near (Isa. 55:1). He is the pursuer.

The sad truth is that even a Christian is not always "near" to God. Just because two people are married does not make them close; a married couple can be estranged in spite of their legal relationship, or they can be intimate, sharing each other's lives and united in heart. Likewise, no words or activity for activity's sake will make us close to God, and even a Christian can neglect the relationship.

Prone to wander, Lord, I feel it,
Prone to leave the God I love.[3]

We must *humble* ourselves to be near him (James 4:7, 10). We must *repent* of our sin (James 4:8b). And we must *seek* him with our "whole heart and soul" (Deut. 4:29 *The Message*). But we usually don't do these things. It is not our habit to humble ourselves; we hang onto our sin, and our tendency is to avoid God like Adam and Eve strung out on apples. We fear judgment, or maybe we think we tried intimacy with God and it did not work out as we hoped, so we settle for a long-distance relationship with God. Even if we honor God with our lips, our hearts are far from him (Matt. 15:8).

What can shake us from this lonely path? What wakes us up to the futility of our false gods and leads us back to intimacy with the one true vine? Often, it is pain.

When troubles come and all these awful things happen to you,
in future days you will come back to GOD, your God,
and listen obediently to what he says. (Deut. 4:30 The Message)

4

In Ezekiel's day, God told idolaters that when they called after idols, God himself would answer and set his face against them, cutting them off from his people (Ezek. 14:8). Why would he do that? To be rid of idolaters once and for all? No, God would do that to draw them *near*: "I will do this to recapture the hearts of the people of Israel" (Ezek. 14:5a).

As God led the Israelites out of Egypt, he took care of their every need. Time and again, however, the Israelites turned their back on their provider, and God would use adversity to draw them back: "When He slew them, *then* they sought Him; and they returned and sought earnestly for God" (Ps. 78:34 NKJV; italics added). God allowed the pain, or sometimes even sent it, to draw his people *near*.

God does not speak to us only through pain, of course. Paul writes that the *kindness* of God can lead us to repentance (Rom. 2:4). But we do not always hear kindness. Our ears can be distracted when God speaks to us through blessings. When we prosper, we may feel like we do not need God after all, that we are doing quite well on our own. Why submit when we are healthy and employed, when we have all we need? What need is there for a Savior when we see nothing from which we need to be saved? So, according to C. S. Lewis, God uses our trials to cut through the deafening noise of success: "God whispers to us in our pleasures, speaks in our conscience, but shouts in our pain: it is His megaphone to rouse a deaf world."[4]

> "Am I only a God nearby," declares the LORD,
> "and not a God far away?" (Jer. 23:23)

5

Hosea's heartache was a message to God's children, then and today, of how it hurts God when we prostitute ourselves to other gods, be they Baal, or materialism, or power, or self, or religious legalism, or whatever. It was a message of how God longs for us to be near him, but it wasn't his only message. God next instructed Hosea to seek out the wife who left him to demonstrate the way God seeks us (and will take us back) when we stray, out of his deep and perfect love.

"Go again; show love to a woman who is loved by another man and is an adulteress, just as the LORD loves the Israelites though they turn to other gods" (Hosea 3:1 HCSB).

So Hosea bought Gomer back. He paid for the privilege of sharing his life with her again. Fifteen shekels of silver and five bushels of barley ransomed Gomer from the auction block, in a picture of the way blood ransoms us from enslavement to sin. And in one of the most beautiful verses in all of Scripture, Hosea tells Gomer, "You must stay with me for many days, and be faithful to me. Do not have another man, and I will also be faithful to you" (Hosea 3:3 NLV).

That is how God would seek out the Israelites in Hosea's day, who had abandoned God like Gomer had left her husband. God would take them back, but not yet. The Israelites had no desire to be near God, so he would reach them through pain. He would use the Assyrians, who took the Israelites into exile, to reach his people.

In exile, God said, the Israelites will have no king. The sacrifices will fall away. Their home will be taken from them, and they will again be aliens in a foreign land. During that time of suffering, though, they will remember God. They will think back on his providence and how God led them out of Egypt. They will wonder what could ever have possessed them to turn to lifeless stone idols. Their pain will lead them back to their Father.

After their hardships, the Israelites "will return and seek the LORD" (Hosea 3:5). God will gather his scattered people. He will have compassion on No Compassion, and he will say to Not My People that "you are my people" (Hosea 2:23). And Israel will say, "You are my God" (Hosea 2:23). It will be pain that draws God's people back. It will be pain that helps them draw near.

Alistair Begg addressed this point in a sermon I heard on his *Truth for Life* podcast. He likened the way God uses suffering to get our attention to the way a child reacts when he slams his finger in a door or skins a knee. What is the first word out of a child's mouth when he's hurt?

Mommy! (Or, less likely, *Daddy!*) The child calls on someone who will love him.

Likewise, Begg points out, it is when we hurt that we cry out to God: *Father!* Because we are fallen, it may be that the painful moments are the *only* times we remember that we need him.

> Let us draw near to God with a sincere heart and with the full assurance that faith brings, having our hearts sprinkled to cleanse us from a guilty conscience and having our bodies washed with pure water. (Heb. 10:22)

6

The book of Hosea never speaks directly of Gomer's pain, but I believe she suffered, too. Yes, her own decisions may have put her in the trial, but it was no less a trial. How many times must she have regretted leaving her children? How many times must she have been wracked with guilt? I believe that she was deeply disappointed in the new life she carved out for herself, or else she would not have been so receptive to Hosea's kindness.

Earlier in this chapter, we heard from betrayed spouses, but the spouses who strayed speak of great pain, too.

> "I would never have thought that I had it in me to cause so much hurt. I didn't feel loved in my marriage, but the way I tried to fix that made me feel like I shouldn't be loved."

The guilt, the disappointment in himself or herself, can isolate a person even further from friends and family, and from God.

> "Living alone, on the edge of divorce, not seeing the kids, too much time to think about what I had done: For a long time, I could not bear to turn to God. Why would he want me? . . ."

But sometimes that same pain can lead to repentance and forgiveness.

> "... But then I thought of the prodigal son. It took humility and pigs and peapods to turn that guy around, and when he did, the Father was there waiting. Maybe, I thought, he would be waiting for me, too."

The suffering can wake a person up and lead to a U-turn.

> "If I had it to do over again, I wouldn't. But the way I understand grace now, the way I treasure forgiveness and God's love, I would not trade it for anything. I just wish I could have learned the lesson another way."

In a sense, the cheating spouses had done to God exactly what they had done to their husbands and wives: they had chased after other "lovers." God used their pain to soften their hearts toward him, and sometimes toward their spouses.

He can do the same for you. The pain of infidelity, like other suffering, hurts to our core, but God can use that pain to do something fantastic. He can use that pain to quicken our hearts and lead us to seek him.

And find him.

> *Come, let us return to the LORD. He has torn us to pieces*
> *but he will heal us; he has injured us*
> *but he will bind up our wounds. (Hosea 6:1)*

7

The next time you are hurting, once you get the "why me" questions out of your system, ask whether this trial can lead you to draw near to God. Have you "Gomered" yourself? Have you pulled away? Has prosperity deafened your ears to God's call? God can use your pain to pull you near, where you can bear fruit and where your joy will be complete. You were not created to be No Compassion or Not My People, and the suffering you endure today can lead you back to God where you can find compassion, where he will call you his child. After all, if you find yourself far from God, he wasn't the one who moved.

In our church recently, there was one couple who stood out as just being joyful. They were visibly moved by the praise hymns. As we sang about God's faithfulness, they looked like they actually believed it. As we sang about God's love, they looked like they actually felt it. I could see the emotion on their faces, and I could see—everyone could see—that this couple was having church in a way that the rest of us were not.

I pointed them out to my wife. We both recognized the couple. I whispered that I wondered what was going on in their life. Sonya said, "Oh, so-and-so just had a miscarriage. Another one."

And I understood. It was because they had just gone through a storm that they were so emphatically sure that God was with them.

And I was ashamed, because why should it even be noticeable when someone is happy to be in church? If the entire congregation had been joyful just to be in the presence of God, as we surely should have been, then this couple would not have stood out at all. But God is not surprised by human nature, and he knows that sometimes only suffering can help us be thankful for our blessings, that only pain can help us remember to turn to him.

---

*I'll be satisfied as long
As I walk, let me walk close to Thee.*[5]

Notes

1. "Near to the Heart of God," Cleland B. McAfee, 1903.
2. Ethel Mae and Talitha Cumi sound almost good compared to Hosea's kids' names.
3. "Come, Thou Fount of Every Blessing," Robert Robinson, 1757.

WHY ME? (And Why That's the Wrong Question)

4. C. S. Lewis, *The Problem of Pain* (New York: HarperCollins, 1940), 91.
5. "Just a Closer Walk with Thee," Anonymous.

Chapter 10

HOW CAN THIS TRIAL HELP ME BECOME MORE LIKE JESUS?

God promises to work all things for good in the life of a believer, but he has a specific "good" in mind. His plan is to make us more like Jesus, and suffering is a tool he uses to change our hearts.

1

"I can't start over," he told me. "I don't know how to do anything else. I don't know how to *be* anything else."

Ron lost his job in 2009. All through 2010 and 2011 he waited, hoping for someone to hire him, but middle managers in their middle fifties were not in demand. Especially in banking.

The family avoided bankruptcy by slashing their spending, and that cut right to the core of Ron's self-image. The Lexus was gone. Summer vacations were things of photographs and videos, not something to be enjoyed in the present. Dining out and the latest fashions, once a given, were now luxuries they could not afford.

"We live a completely different life now," he said, "but the ego blow was harder than the financial adjustment. The whole 'man must provide' thing eats at me, and that affects Lucy, too."

"I'm scared," he said, and the tone of voice made me believe him. "I don't know what to do. I'm not even sure who I am without the job and without the life that went with it."

We are transfigured by the Spirit of the Lord in ever-increasing splendour into his own image. (2 Cor. 3:18b PHILLIPS)

2

Millions lost their jobs during the Great Recession that began in 2007, and as of this writing, unemployment is still too high. The trial of financial insecurity can shake a family to its core, especially if, like Ron, they have looked to money and possessions for security.

Some live in fear. Anxiety would be perfectly normal during a time of rapid change, but the fear I'm talking about is a paralyzing fear that lasts as long as the economic hardship. Others, like Ron, eventually learn to respond in a different way.

A year or so after the conversation I related above, Ron found work in his industry. The new job was in a small local bank without all the perks and prestige of the large national bank he used to work for, but he will tell you he was one of the lucky ones.

Finding a job, any job, was a relief, but that was not the best thing to come out of the experience. As a result of his period of unemployment and the adjustment in lifestyle, Ron stopped looking to money and status for his security, and he learned lessons about God's provision that will last for the rest of his life.

"I never had one of those moments you hear about, when you're sitting at the kitchen table wondering how you will pay a bill for $217, and then the mailman brings a check for exactly $217. God's provision for us was not so instant or precise, but he did provide. The beautiful thing for us was that over time, I started to see money in a completely different way. I learned that I belonged to God whether I had a job or not. He loved me whether we had one car or two. My value came from being in Christ, not in my toys or whether people thought of me as successful. I can't believe how shallow I was.

"I make a lot less now than I did before, but I care a lot less about that now. Being out of work changed me. *God* changed me."

For we are God's handiwork, created in Christ Jesus to do good works, which God prepared in advance for us to do. (Eph. 2:10)

3

If God is the potter and we are the clay, suffering is often the tool he uses to shape us. That shaping and molding is a lifelong process. There is a tremendous change that happens in a moment when we are saved and receive a new spirit, when God removes our heart of stone and gives us a heart of flesh (Ezek. 11:19; 18:31; 36:26). Sanctification, though—God's work of making us more like Christ—is a process that continues until we die. And I bet that if you look back, the times when you grew the most were not the easy times, but the tough ones.

Think of the times in the Bible when a person was called to service, but the real work began only after a period of hardship. The hardship was used to equip the person to be God's man or woman. Paul, after his dramatic call on the road to Damascus, had to sneak out of a window and practically hide for years before he was ready to give up his desire to be God's missionary to the Jews. Only then could he follow God's call to take the gospel to the Gentile world. Joseph was prideful and manipulative in his pretty coat, but after he was sold into slavery and wrongfully imprisoned, he learned forgiveness and humility. Moses spent forty years in obscurity (after running from a murder rap) before he was ready to face Pharaoh. Jonah spent three days in the belly of a fish before he decided to obey God's call. God used suffering to shape Paul, Joseph, Moses, and Jonah, to form them into people fit for service and leadership and missions.

He can do the same for us. God may take us as we are, but he has no intention of leaving us that way. And there is no randomness, not a bit, to God's design for our lives. He molds us to the pattern of his Son. In fact, that is God's plan for our lives: to make us like Jesus.

There is a well-known verse often quoted in a trial: "And we know that all things work together for good to those who love God, to those who are the called according to *His* purpose" (Rom. 8:28 NKJV). That does *not* mean that every trial will have a happy ending as we define it, though that is often how the verse is misused. It does not mean that if you lose your job, God has promised that you will find another one just as good as the old one, or even that you will find another job at all. The "good" that will always work out is defined by the next verse, which is not quoted so often: "For whom He foreknew, He also predestined to be *conformed to the image of His Son*, that He might be the firstborn among many brethren" (Rom. 8:29 NKJV; italics added).

Do you see? God does not promise that everything will always work out okay on our terms. He does not promise our choice of "good." The good he promises is that if we let him, he can use any trial to make us more like Jesus.

Think about it: God's definition of "good" is *himself*, and Jesus is the image of the Father (John 14:9). Making us more like him is the best thing that can happen to us, and this is what he promises. He does this in at least four ways: through discipline, with pruning shears, by proving our faith, and by giving us knowledge of the sufferings of Christ.

I am the true vine, and my Father is the vinedresser. Every branch in me that does not bear fruit he takes away. (John 15:1–2a ESV)

4

Discipline

Parents understand discipline. Loving parents do not enjoy it, but it is necessary for the good of their children. We use stern actions to protect them, to help them understand not to run into the street or touch a hot stove, and to help them develop moral character. This is godly parenting (Prov. 13:24). Likewise, God loves us and disciplines us for our good. "The LORD reproves him whom he loves, as a father the son in whom he delights" (PROV. 3:12 ESV).

At the time we were sitting in a corner or sent to our rooms as children, we probably did not appreciate our parents' discipline. We did not realize then that it was for our own good and that it was proof of our parents' love. As adults, though, especially if we have kids of our own, we can look back and appreciate what our parents did to shape us and keep us safe.

God's discipline is the same. If we have strayed—if we are doing things we shouldn't, or failing to do things we should—God can use trials to correct us. Just as when we went through our parents' discipline, we may not enjoy it or even understand God's discipline at the time, but in the end we can be grateful for the result. And, like our parents, he does it all out of love. In fact, if he did not love us, God would not discipline us at all: "Those whom I love, I reprove and discipline, so be zealous and repent" (Rev. 3:19 ESV).

We are *blessed* if God disciplines us (Job 5:17–18; Ps. 94:12–13). It is proof that we belong to him, and it is something that all his legitimate children experience. "God is treating you as sons. For what son is there whom his father does not discipline? . . . For the moment all discipline seems painful rather than pleasant, but later it yields the peaceful fruit of righteousness to those who have been trained by it" (Heb. 12:7, 11 ESV).

Bruce Wilkinson treats the subject of discipline beautifully. In *Secrets of the Vine*, Wilkinson dissects Jesus' discussion of the vine and the branches in John 15.[1] There Jesus says we must be connected to him to bear fruit. If a branch in Christ—a person who is saved—is not bearing fruit, the vinedresser (God the Father) "takes away" or "cuts off" that branch, according to most English translations (John 15:2). That wording suggests that someone connected to the vine could lose his or her salvation and be discarded by God, but the Bible says that nothing can ever snatch us from the Shepherd's hand (John 10:28) and that nothing can separate us from the love of Christ (Rom. 8:35–39).

Wilkinson believes that a better translation of Jesus' words would be "to lift up."[2] The picture is of God lovingly, tenderly caring for the branch, lifting it off the ground and cleaning it so that it is not choked by dirt and grime. God wants that branch to bear fruit, not to burn, so he gives the branch what it needs, even if it is temporarily painful to the branch.

So what does God's discipline look like? Does he *send* hardship our way? Or does he sometimes, to get our attention, choose not to grant our prayer for deliverance but instead *allow* a trial to endure? It is hard to say for any specific circumstance. There are times in the Old Testament when God raises up a people to take the Israelites into exile because of their sin, and it seems that God is the cause of a trial. The trial would not have occurred if God had not acted affirmatively. And the Bible tells of discipline that may seem harsh to us. Paul refers to the fact that some Corinthians were allowed to endure sickness and even death because they observed the Lord's Supper in "an unworthy manner" (1 Cor. 11:27–32). As with all suffering, there are mysteries as to how exactly God works in the area of discipline. Whether the trial used to discipline us is sent or permitted, we can know God is acting in love. And besides, if we are being disciplined, the *source* of the trial is not as important as its *purpose* or the *result* God intends.

And how do we know if we are being disciplined? I can offer a theory, but that's all it is; I have no Scripture that backs this up. If God is using a trial to mold my character, I cannot believe he would be cagey about it. That would defeat the purpose. He will let me know, I believe, because he desires that I change my behavior or thinking in some way. (Nor do I believe he would discipline me by causing pain to someone else; if my trial is watching someone *else* go through pain, that trial can still be used to mold my character, but I think we would have to classify it as something other than discipline of *me*.)

If we are unsure whether a hardship is God's discipline, we should ask him. If we wonder whether a storm is being used to get our attention, we can ask God to point out areas in our lives that we should change, then make the change and see if the trial ends.

Once we see that it is fruitless to speculate about the precise mechanics of discipline (whether God sends the hardship or merely allows it), and once we have faith that God will let us know when he is using a hardship to mold our character, we can focus on the result that God desires. And the result is good. The author of Psalm 119, traditionally thought to be David, wrote of the positive effects of God's discipline. "Before I was afflicted," the author writes, "I went astray, but now I keep Your word.... It was good for me to be afflicted so that I could learn Your statutes" (Ps. 119:67, 71 HCSB). He strayed from God—he sinned—but a time of hardship brought him back to God's Word. The pain hurt, but the result was "good."

Has financial security become your god? Are you pursuing a relationship that is out of bounds? Has bitterness, envy, or an unforgiving spirit sapped you of any enthusiasm for the kingdom of God? Unconfessed sin can make you a barren branch. God may discipline you at such times to get you back on track.

This does not mean that every time you suffer it is because you have done something wrong. We've already dealt with that. God never says that *all* suffering is discipline, but *some* suffering is. It will be unpleasant at the time, but if we submit to God's discipline, we become more like his Son, and we will have further proof of his love for us. We can know that we are his children, and our barren branches will begin to bear fruit.

> *... and every branch that does bear fruit he prunes,*
> *that it may bear more fruit. (John 15:2b ESV)*

5

Pruning

There is discipline for the branch that is bearing no fruit, but the vinedresser *prunes* the branch that is bearing a little fruit and could be more productive (John 15:2). It's not that we're going down the wrong path entirely, but if we just cleaned a few things up—if we reduced or got rid of unproductive thoughts and activities—we could be producing *more* fruit.

Gardeners understand pruning. When I was a kid, our family had muscadine and scuppernong vines, wild grapes that grow in the South. We would cut the plants back periodically until it looked like there was no way the vines would survive. All the frilly, pretty parts would be gone, and we would be left with a bare main vine and a few sturdy branches. Those years would provide a bumper crop. And lots of jelly.

If we did not prune the vines, they would be full and leafy and beautifully green, but the fruit would be scarcer. There would be some fruit to pick, but not as much as you would think when the vines looked so healthy. Roses are the same way, as well as the crepe myrtles in my backyard. The plant can put its energy into leaves and shoots and branches, or into bearing fruit or flowers, but it can't do both.

Even if we are living for Christ, there may still be parts of our lives that, while not necessarily sinful, are unproductive in kingdom terms. When I was first starting my career as a lawyer, we attended church, but I was not involved in ministry. I assumed I did not have time. As a member of a large law firm, I had an active social calendar, I was burning the midnight oil to get ahead, we had season tickets to watch our favorite football team, and God could just be happy with whatever I had left over (so I thought).

Over time, I developed a sense of discontentment with where I was in my Christian walk. The things that had made me happy, or that I had thought would be good for me in the long run, left me unfulfilled. My life was full of fun things or career-building activities, and none of them was sinful in and of itself, but they left me no time for activity in church beyond attending. I began paring back a little here and there—I didn't have to watch *all* of those shows, or go to *all* the games, or work late *quite* as much—until there was time to volunteer to teach a Bible study class. And I've been teaching since that day.

I had been pruned. I can't point to a particular trial or period of suffering that God used to prune me, other than a general feeling of dissatisfaction (which I do not consider to be "suffering"), but God had sheared me nonetheless. He lopped off the leafy branch that was watching almost every Braves game, and we let the season tickets lapse (one or two games a year would do).[3] He clipped a little of the drive to do extra work solely out of selfish ambition and the desire for approval. More energy was devoted to productive activities, and I produced more fruit.

There are all kinds of areas God might trim. Exercise, for instance, is not sinful. It's good to take care of our bodies. But a person can become obsessed with exercise until it eats up far more of her schedule than necessary for a healthy lifestyle. Providing for our families is necessary, but take it too far, and we are little more than our job. Sports, shopping, hobbies, leisure activities, video games, or time online can all become leafy, fruitless branches that God seeks to prune, and a trial can be the shears he uses to grab our attention and ask us to cut back or let go.

Ron, from the story at the beginning of this chapter, was pruned of his dependence on possessions. Paul was pruned of his reliance on a Jewish education and pedigree and learned to count those things as trash (Phil. 3:8). What might God prune from your life?

As Wilkinson notes, pruning may at times feel a lot like discipline, but the goal and result are different. Discipline seeks to change wrongful behavior and to take us from no fruit to some fruit; pruning is when God seeks to limit certain behavior that may not be sinful but saps energy that could be used in better ways.[4] Suffering can be God's tool in either, and either will make us more like Christ.

> *I have refined you, but not as silver is refined. Rather, I have refined you in the furnace of suffering. (Isa. 48:10 NLT)*

6

Testing of Our Faith

God can also use suffering to test your faith and prove that it is real. The picture is that of fire refining fine metals, burning out the impurities.

When it was time to enter the Promised Land, Moses spoke to the Israelites about their time in the wilderness. It was a punishment the Israelites brought upon themselves forty years earlier when they refused to trust God to help them conquer the land. Moses reminded the people how God used that time in the desert. The people were wholly dependent upon God for every bite of food and every drop of water (so are we; it was just more obvious to the Israelites). God provided water from a rock and manna from heaven, and he built his people's faith. Moses said, "You shall remember all the way which the LORD your God has led you in the wilderness these forty years, that He might humble you, testing you, to know what was in your heart, whether you would keep His commandments or not" (Deut. 8:2 NASB). The testing in the desert showed their faith.

Zechariah prophesied that fire (suffering) would purify and lead a people to call on God (Zech. 13:9). Through Malachi, God said that he would refine the Levites like gold and silver so that they would bring offerings in righteousness (Mal. 3:3). When your faith is tested, it reveals what is in your heart and can *change* your heart.

Abraham believed God's promises, but his faith was still tested. God promised that Abraham would have many descendants through his miracle child Isaac, and Abraham's belief was credited to him as righteousness (Gen. 15:6). So what did Abraham think when God asked him to sacrifice Isaac? Abraham knew that somehow, some way, Isaac would come back down the mountain. After all, God promised that Isaac would give Abraham grandchildren, so if God was going to keep that promise, Isaac must somehow survive. Abraham knew this in his core, so he was obedient to the final moment when God (in a foreshadowing of Jesus) provided a substitute sacrifice (Heb. 11:17–19; Gen. 22:1–14).

Who was this test for? God already knew the level of Abraham's faith. He knows everything. I believe that, in addition to the inspiration the story would give those who read the Bible, God wanted *Abraham* to know how strong his faith was. That knowledge gave Abraham security and certainty of his standing with God. When we make it through a trial without losing faith, we can say, "With God's help, this trial did not defeat me. I *can* trust him, and I *do*." Being certain of a little faith can *increase* our faith.

The testing of our faith also produces perseverance (James 1:3). When you survive one storm, the next storm does not seem as daunting. It doesn't seem fun, either, but you know you did it once—with God's help—and you can do it again. Knowing this helps you press on.

So how does this demonstration of faith make us more like Jesus? If our faith has been shown as real to us, then perhaps we will be more willing to obey God's commands. Let's face it: sometimes God's commands point in the opposite direction of where we think we should go. Last to be first? Weak to be strong? Lose our life to keep it? Through our human eyes, some of what the Bible says is counterintuitive. But if we have made it through trials, if our faith has been tested, we are more likely to obey (to behave like Jesus) even when it doesn't make sense: *I don't see how this can be the right move, but God says it is, and I believe him.* No, we do not know how the trial will end, whether by divine deliverance or even death, but we can know that it will not separate us from the love of Christ.

Consider the mind of Christ when he was entering the storm. He did not turn his back on the Father. He did not avoid the crucifixion, even though he wished very much that another path was possible. He submitted to God's will and rested in the Father's love even when forsaken for our sins. Instead of cursing God, Jesus praised him. Instead of fleeing from God, Jesus ran to his embrace. This is the way that, through God's grace, we too can respond to trials, and it's all the easier if we have the evidence of making it through an earlier trial.

But rejoice inasmuch as you participate in the sufferings of Christ, so that you may be overjoyed when his glory is revealed.
(1 Pet. 4:13)

7
Sharing in Jesus' Suffering

Lastly, God can use trials to make us more like Christ because they allow us to share in Jesus' suffering and know him more intimately. This was Paul's earnest desire. He said, "I want to know Christ and the power of his resurrection and the fellowship of sharing in his sufferings, becoming like him in his death . . ." (Phil. 3:10 NIV 1984).

This does not mean that we join Jesus on the cross, obviously. The whole point of the cross was to take our place. Nor is it masochism. Paul did not seek out pain for pain's sake. He recognized, though, that understanding and sharing in Jesus' suffering will allow us to know Christ better. When we are in pain, we can identify with Christ and feel empathy for what he went through on our behalf.

The goal is not an intellectual understanding of what crucifixion feels like. Paul says that sharing in Jesus' suffering leads to "attaining to the resurrection from the dead" (Phil. 3:11). It isn't the pain itself that leads to eternal life, but the fellowship with Jesus, and this fellowship is enhanced through a better understanding of his suffering.

Fellowship doesn't always have to hurt, of course. But Paul saw in his own suffering the opportunity to identify with the Suffering Servant, to better understand Jesus' heartache. As with any relationship, shared experience with Christ draws us closer to him.

The shared experience also allows us better to appreciate the price that Jesus paid. This makes us grateful, or it should. And that gratitude can quicken our desire to please him through obedience. Right behavior spurred in this way is not a futile attempt to gain salvation, but a love offering. Because suffering allows us to identify with the sufferings of Jesus, we know and love him more, and this makes us more like him.

You also, like living stones, are being built into a spiritual house to be a holy priesthood. (1 Pet. 2:5)

8

If you are hurting, God may be working to change you. Whether the trial is the direct result of sin or was completely beyond your control, and whether the trial was sent by God or was something he merely permitted, God can use it to encourage you to take a look in the mirror.

Discipline, pruning, faith-testing, and sharing in Christ's suffering are tools that God uses to make us into the image of his Son. That's how God transformed Ron. Ron's entire attitude about money and possessions was changed because of a trial, and he learned to look to God for his security and to store up treasures in heaven. For us it could be a sinful habit, an attitude, a dependence, or neglectfulness.

WHY ME? (And Why That's the Wrong Question)

If recession has hit your family, you may have wondered why you lost your job and another person did not, or you may want to ask why God has left you to fend for yourself (or so it may seem to you). Ask away, and take your questions to God.

Don't stop there, though. Move on to other questions, and consider how God might use this trial to change your behavior, mold your character, or increase your faith.

A storm can push us to let go of something that is holding us back. God has a plan to make you more and more like Jesus each day, and he "will continue his work until it is finally finished on the day when Christ Jesus returns" (Phil. 1:6 NLT).

Notes

1. Bruce Wilkinson, *Secrets of the Vine* (Colorado Springs: Multnomah, 2001).
2. Ibid., 34–39. The Greek word translated as "take away" in this verse (*airei*) can indeed mean to take away, but it can also mean to "elevate" or "lift up." It is the same Greek word used in Matthew 4:6, where Satan tempts Jesus with Scripture, saying that the angels will "lift him up."
3. I still watch all the football games on TV. Even the ones on pay-per-view against Northwest South Carolina A&M Tech Institute. I really, really hope the pruning shears stay far away from that branch.
4. Wilkinson, *Secrets*, 63–67.

Chapter 11

HOW CAN I GLORIFY GOD IN MY SUFFERING?

God commands us to give him glory, and he deserves it. One good thing about a trial is that it gives us many ways to fulfill this commandment. God's care for us, our response to suffering, and what we share with others can all glorify him.

1
Worst. Parents. *Ever.*

Our son Tully had just started first grade. It was not entirely what he expected, and he had a few imaginary tummyaches when he realized how much school would cut into his free time. So when he again said that his stomach hurt one Friday morning—and he was fever-free and ate breakfast—we ignored it and sent him to school.

Saturday he complained again about the pain. There being no school to avoid, we had to admit that there might be something behind the complaints. At most, though, it was probably the bug going around. A little juice, a little TLC, check his temperature, and wait it out.

Sunday night, he was running a fever. We left a message with the pediatrician to make an appointment for the next day.

By Monday morning, he was nearly unresponsive. His fever was higher, he would not eat or drink, and we knew it was serious. What we spent three days practically ignoring took the pediatrician about thirty seconds to diagnose: our son's appendix was inflamed and possibly ruptured. We went straight to Children's Hospital. The doctor's urgency, calling ahead to a surgeon, panicked us. We did not even have time to feel guilty about being such terrible, no-good, clueless, deaf, and blind caregivers who obviously had no business taking care of a child.

Tully just turned fifteen, so obviously it all worked out. An infected appendix, or even a ruptured one (like Tully's turned out to be), is not nearly as serious as what many of the other kids in the hospital were dealing with. At that moment, though, Sonya and I were as terrified as we had ever been. We watched people in surgical masks take our child away. We held each other, helpless, and waited.

We prayed. We talked to God a lot that day. We *needed* him. And we knew that as believers, we should glorify God in all things. To be honest, though, the thought of glorifying God never once crossed my mind as I sat in the waiting room.

Begging, yes. Praising? Not so much.

Ascribe to the LORD the glory due his name;
worship the LORD in the splendor of his holiness. (Ps. 29:2)

2

I think God will excuse me for being preoccupied during my son's surgery. I think he understands if there are moments in the day when I am not exalting him out loud. Nonetheless, we are called to glorify God in *all* that we do, including our actions and attitudes, and trials give us fantastic opportunities to do just that. Even if my mind is centered on a crisis, I can respond to that crisis in a way that glorifies him, and I can be glad for the glory that comes as a result of the trial.

Glorifying God is our duty and privilege. In fact, some say, it is the reason we are here. In the sixteen hundreds, English and Scottish theologians met and produced a document summarizing their beliefs. The *Westminster Shorter Catechism* begins in this way:

Q. What is the chief end of man?
A. Man's chief end is to glorify God, and to enjoy him forever.

Maybe they were right. A lot of people have thought so over the years. Or maybe, instead, God's greatest desire is that we *love* him and *obey* him (Deut. 6), and God is glorified as a result of our love and obedience. I'll let the theologians sort out whether God seeks his glory as an end in itself, because nothing is more important to him than his own glory, or whether he mainly wants us to love and obey, and his glorification is the natural result of love and obedience. Either way, we are undeniably called to bring glory to God.

God is perfect and holy and deserves to be glorified (Rev. 4:11). He gave us life, and he loves us in spite of our rebellion. The heavens shout his glory (Ps. 19:1). The beasts of the field give him honor (Isa. 43:20). The angels sing his praises (Isa. 6:3). Why should we be different?

When we speak of giving glory to God, it doesn't mean that we have some glory, and we are taking some from ourselves and adding to what God has. God already has all the glory he can ever possess. He is glorious to infinity, and nothing we say or do can give him any more glory than he already has. This intrinsic glory is the "glory of the Lord" that looked like a burning fire on top of the mountain to Moses and the Israelites (Exod. 24:17), and that passed by as Moses sheltered in the cleft of the rock (Exod. 33:22).

Here, the glory we give to God means the honor and adoration that we offer him. We are not giving him a magnificence he does not already possess; we are instead recognizing and acknowledging how great he is (and making that known to others). Thus the command to "ascribe to" him the "glory due his name" (Ps. 29:2) and to "extol" him with our mouths (Ps. 109:30). And there are *lots* of ways to do that.

We glorify him with our words when we speak of his greatness and when we appreciate his worth and adore him (Ps. 100:2). God is glorified when we acknowledge Jesus Christ as Lord (Phil. 2:11). We also glorify God through obedience to his law: Paul's prayer for the Philippians was that they would be wise in knowing how to behave and that they would be filled with righteousness, because this would be "to the glory and praise of God" (Phil. 1:9–11).

God is glorified when we long for his company, when we care how other people speak of him, when we confess our sin and acknowledge his rightness, when we are content that God's will be done, and when we do not mind other people getting the credit.

We glorify God when we believe what he says, and we dishonor him when we don't (Rom. 4:20). We give him his due when we produce fruit. Back in the vineyard, Jesus said, "My Father is glorified by this: that you produce much fruit and prove to be My disciples" (John 15:8 HCSB). It gives him glory when we are cheerful, when we stand up for truth (Jude 3), when we have zeal for his house (John 2:14–17). And surely we glorify him when we recognize his sovereignty by being satisfied with the life he has laid out for us. "The LORD is my chosen portion and my cup; you hold my lot. The lines have fallen for me in pleasant places; indeed, I have a beautiful inheritance" (Ps. 16:5–6 ESV).

When something happens that only God can do, and people see that God is doing wonderful things, he is glorified. When we are loving to each other, it honors him. Whenever we hold firm to our faith or when we share the gospel, we tell the world, "God is marvelous," and this brings him glory.

This means that you can bring glory to God through the most routine and mundane activities if done for him with a proper attitude. So Paul writes that you should "bring glory to God both in your body and your spirit, for they both belong to him" (1 Cor. 6:20 PHILLIPS). He says that "whether you eat or drink or whatever you do, do it all for the glory of God" (1 Cor. 10:31). And "whatever you do, whether in word or deed, do it all in the name of the Lord Jesus, giving thanks to God the Father through him" (Col. 3:17).[1]

No other person in the universe is worthy of the glory due the triune God, and we should at all times seek to honor him. This fits right in with our study of suffering, because trials present so many opportunities for God to receive glory. He can be glorified through the way he intervenes, the way we respond, and what we tell others.

I am the LORD; that is my name! I will not yield my glory to another or my praise to idols. (Isa. 42:8)

3

One way God can be glorified in our trials—and a way that we should never hesitate to root for—is through a miracle that solves our problem outright. When the Israelites were cornered by the Egyptian army, God was magnified by the Red Sea miracle. God was glorified when Jesus raised Lazarus from the dead, too. When Lazarus was dying, Jesus said, "This sickness will not end in death. No, it is for God's glory so that God's Son may be glorified through it" (John 11:4). And Jesus pointed out how blindness was another opportunity for God to be exalted through miraculous healing (John 9:3–5).

These miracles, and hundreds like them, gave evidence for all to see of God's might and goodness. When the laws of science and nature offer no way out of a situation, but we are delivered nonetheless, we know it is by God's hand. We should rejoice in such times and give the glory to him.

So yes, God can be glorified by the way he intervenes in our trials, but let's not forget the Scriptures we studied in earlier chapters. There are many ways that he can intervene in your trial. If you are blind, sight is the most obvious possible miracle, but it's not the only one. God may instead walk with you in your blindness. He may calm your fears and strengthen you so that you can deal with a disability. God is glorified by this kind of intervention, too.

Paul suffered some type of affliction and prayed that God would take it away. God said no. Instead of healing Paul, God gave him the strength to handle it and said, "My grace is enough; it's all you need. My strength comes into its own in your weakness" (2 Cor. 12:9 *The Message*). And God was glorified by Paul doing mighty things in spite of his affliction.

David wrote that God restores our souls and leads us in the path of righteousness "for His name's sake" (Ps. 23:3 NKJV). Then let's glorify his name, whether he takes away the blindness or leads us by hand.

*Be exalted, O God, above the heavens;
let your glory be over all the earth. (Ps. 57:5)*

4

Say the pink slip comes tomorrow. There are many different ways you could react. You could panic, withdraw from family and friends and church, sit around in sweatpants, and tell the world how unfair God is being after you've been a Christian all your life. How much glory would you say you are giving to God if this is your response? God says we turn "glory into shame" when we run after false gods (Ps. 4:2), and despair and self-indulgence can be false gods.

Or, even though you may be afraid and anxious, you can still behave in a way that magnifies God's name. You might do that by leaning on God instead of running from him, remaining grateful for God's blessings, keeping up your tithe in hard times, testifying to the goodness of God, and showing the world that you still trust in God's provision.

I don't mean that we should put on a false face and hide our true feelings. We do no good to anyone by pretending that Christians don't have problems. Instead, we can show the world that in the midst of our pain and questions, we still trust God and love him; that we don't despair or give up hope at every bump in the road; that we trust that somehow, in the way he sees best, God will see us through the trial. We can thus give God glory through our *response* to a trial, no matter what the *outcome*.

When Paul wrote to the Christians in Thessalonica, he told them their response to trials—in that case, the death of a loved one—should not be the same as people who do not know God: "Brothers and sisters, we do not want you to be uninformed about those who sleep in death, so that you do not grieve like the rest of mankind, who have no hope" (1 Thess. 4:13). He then goes on to teach them that those in Christ will rise again in the last day and live with him forever.

Note that Paul does not say a Christian should not grieve, period. Of course we grieve if a friend or family member dies. Paul says instead that we should not grieve *in the same manner* as someone who has no hope. There is a difference between sadness and hopelessness, and grief is not the same as giving up. *In* our grief and sadness, we can remember that death is not final. We can remember that because Jesus died, we live, and because he rose again, we live with him. We don't have to act like we have no hope, because we *do* have hope.

Because we have hope, we don't give up on life when we're hurting. We keep up our time with God and talk to him about our frustrations and even our anger, but we do talk to him. And when we tell him how we feel, we can also tell him that we love him even though we do not understand why the loss has happened. We show that we believe in the gospel even when we feel like dying. We are thankful for God's love, although we certainly are not thankful that a funeral was necessary, and when thanksgiving overflows, God is glorified (2 Cor. 4:15).

Consider this: When people watch you during a trial, do they see any evidence that you have faith in God's promises? When people see that you have hope, they may want some of that hope for themselves. They may wonder how it is that you can carry on and how the bleakness of your situation has not broken you. When you tell them that God's grace is enough, God is glorified.

> *Even every one that is called by my name: for I have created him for my glory, I have formed him; yea, I have made him. (Isa. 43:7 KJV)*

5

We can also glorify God in our suffering by the way he transforms us. In the last chapter, we discussed how God can use trials to make us more like Jesus. When we are more like Jesus, we reflect him, to his glory. "All of us, with no covering on our faces, show the shining-greatness of the Lord as in a mirror. All the time we are being changed to look like Him, with more and more of His shining-greatness" (2 Cor. 3:18 NLV). Like the moon reflects the sun, we reflect the glory of Christ to a world that needs to see him, his glory, his "shining-greatness."

That scares me sometimes, because if we can reflect his goodness, we can also reflect poorly. My bad behavior can give people a bad impression of Jesus. But that fear makes me more conscious of how I respond to bad news. When we are loving, we are more like him and the world can see his glory. When we are not—when our response to pain is to be selfish and petty and grumpy and greedy—people look at us and wonder whether being a Christian makes any difference.

No one will *always* give a positive image of Christ, except Christ himself. But we come closer and closer to that standard as God molds us through suffering. As we reflect his righteousness, we are shown to be "the work of [God's] hands, that [he] may be glorified" (Isa. 60:21 NASB).

> *For of Him and through Him and to Him are all things, to whom be glory forever. Amen. (Rom. 11:36 NKJV)*

6

We also give honor to God by telling others what he has done for us. If God heals you, or if he makes a problem go away, give him the glory and let people know what a wondrous thing God has done in your life.

But as we have discussed, God is at work in your trial whether or not he heals you or solves the immediate problem. He is at work if he props up your spirit and gives you the strength to keep going. Share that, too. Tell others how God used your trial to bring you closer to him and make you more like his Son.

If God does something great for you, don't keep it to yourself. Christians want to rejoice with you and will be encouraged by your testimony, and non-Christians will see evidence of God's power and goodness. There is a public component of glorification, and sitting on your good news will help no one. "One generation shall praise Your works to another, And shall declare Your mighty acts" (Ps. 145:4 NKJV).

Glory to God in the highest heaven. (Luke 2:14a)

7

What if your suffering ends in death? Can God still be glorified? I think so, if we face death as one who knows that Jesus has prepared a place for us. When Jesus prophesied that Peter would be martyred for his faith, John wrote, "Jesus said this to indicate the kind of death by which Peter would *glorify* God" (John 21:19; italics added).

We do not choose the time and manner we leave this world, but we do choose an attitude toward death. The deaths of the early Christian martyrs were grisly and horrible, but they were good deaths because Paul, Peter, and the gang faced death with courage and with anticipation of heaven.

Except for Judas Iscariot (suicide) and John (old age), all the disciples were murdered for preaching the gospel. James, John's brother, is the only disciple whose execution is noted in the Bible (Acts 12:2), but history and tradition say that the others died in equally horrific ways. And they faced it with faith.

James supposedly shared the gospel on the way to his beheading. Peter, forced to watch his wife's death before his own crucifixion, reputedly urged his wife to "Remember the Lord!" as she died. (And Peter supposedly asked to be crucified upside down because he felt unworthy to die in the same fashion as Jesus.)[2] Stephen, the first recorded post-ascension martyr, preached at his own trial, and God's glory was on his lips as the stones flew (Acts 7).

These deaths gave glory to God. Even if our last words do not involve witnessing, we can face death in the same manner as these giants of the faith. That doesn't mean we should seek it out, or pretend that an untimely death does not involve regrets, or pretend that we don't wish it would come a little later. It does mean that we can face it as if we believe the gospel, as if we believe that the death of Christ was indeed sufficient to pay for our sins, and as if we believe that he rose again and will do the same for us. If we really believe these things, shouldn't that make a difference in how we view death?

Look, I don't want to die any time soon. There is a lot left to do. I want to see the pyramids. I want to go to Africa and Alaska. I want to see how George R. R. Martin finishes his *Song of Ice and Fire* series. I want to see my son grow into manhood and possibly have children of his own, and I want to do all this growing old with Sonya. If I found out tomorrow that I had a year to live, I would grieve and maybe feel sorry for myself. But only for a time, I hope. I hope that after the shock, I would remember the promises of God. There would be disappointment for the places and people and things I will not experience in this world, but those regrets should be overshadowed by the hope of the glory to come. If I faced death that way, looking forward to heaven even in my sadness, then my death would glorify God.

Remember Daniel's friends Shadrach, Meshach, and Abednego? They had a choice: worship Nebuchadnezzar's false idol, or die in a blazing furnace. They chose God. They told the King:

> If the God we serve exists, then He can rescue us from the furnace of blazing fire, and He can rescue us from the power of you, the king. But even if He does not rescue us, we want you as king to know that we will not serve your gods or worship the gold statue you set up. (Dan. 3:17–18 HCSB)

But even if he does not. God could save them, the boys knew, but whether he did or not, they would keep faith. They were prepared to glorify God even in their death. They were prepared to "glorify ye the LORD in the fires" (Isa. 24:15 KJV).

I glorified thee on the earth, having accomplished the work which thou hast given me to do. (John 17:4 ASV)

8

Tully came through his appendectomy like a champ. The situation was not nearly as serious as it seemed at first, but as I said before, we were terrified at the time. Scared enough that I had no conscious thought of how I could glorify God, which I think is okay under the circumstances. Looking back, though, how could I have glorified God during Tully's illness and hospitalization? Through many different ways, such as:

- being pleasant to the medical staff;
- showing love to the other parents hanging out, most of whom were there under far more serious circumstances;
- acknowledging my dependence on God, both to myself and, if it came up, to other parents in conversation;
- not letting our human fear for Tully's safety control us;

- staying close to Sonya so that we could minister to each other;
- allowing the trial to motivate me to be a better dad;
- showing gratitude to God for the successful treatment and praising him publicly.

It's not rocket science. The items on this list are things anyone can do, although I don't claim to have done them all very well. For this chapter's purposes, the importance of the list is that these were opportunities for me to glorify God that never would have occurred without the trial.

Don't get me wrong. If I had a million chances to avoid the situation entirely, I would avoid it a million times. It was my son, after all. But it *did* happen, and one good thing that resulted is that God was glorified.

Now to the King eternal, immortal, invisible, the only God, be honor and glory for ever and ever. Amen. (1 Tim. 1:17)

9

Your next trial may be more serious than a bad appendix. It may give you good reason to be scared and anxious. You should pray that God will intervene to heal you, or fix the relationship, or provide another job. He may do just that and be glorified by doing so. Or, he may intervene by giving you strength, or sending others to comfort you, and be glorified by doing so.

No one can guarantee the outcome of your trial or how God will answer prayer. What I can guarantee is this: your trial will involve lots of ways for God to be glorified. He will take care of you and see you through it. You can respond gracefully and with faith, and you can tell others all that God has done for you. It won't stop the hurting, but it is a blessing all its own that through your pain, the magnificence of the living God will be reflected in you, put on display to a hurting world.

Notes

1. I called my sister once after she had studied these passages. She said she was "dusting for Jesus."
2. John MacArthur, *Twelve Ordinary Men* (Nashville: Thomas Nelson, 2002), 60.

MY JOURNEY TO JOY

The following testimony by Marie Hillstrom describes the way God worked in her family's life as she and her husband faced the challenge of raising daughters with special needs. Marie asked all the right questions and, by the grace of God, found growth and peace and joy in the midst of hardship.

"I hope you're sitting down," our adoption social worker said. "You and two other couples have been selected by a birth mom as potential parents of her infant twins. But there's something important you need to know. She drank alcohol throughout her pregnancy, and we don't know what effect that will have on the children. They'll probably have some learning disabilities. Are you interested?"

"Of course," I blurted out. We'd struggled with infertility for several years, and here was our chance to get not one, but two, babies. "Oh, there's one other thing," our social worker added. "In order to make her decision, the birth mom wants your explanation of how to obtain inner peace."

Later that day, my husband and I met to discuss what to do. "She might think we're crazy and not choose us if we tell her the way to inner peace is through a personal relationship with Jesus Christ," I told Josh. "We can't deny our faith," he replied. "We've got to tell the truth even if it means the adoption doesn't go through."

That night we carefully drafted a short paragraph answering the birth mom's question and gave it to the adoption agency. Then we waited. After a few days, we got our answer. "Are you sitting down?" our social worker said. "You've been chosen to become parents of the twins."

Two weeks later, we drove to a nearby town to pick up our girls. "The birth mom chose you for a specific reason," the county representative said. "While she was pregnant, she lived with a Christian foster family. They showed her a love she'd never known, so she wanted Christians to adopt her children."

It seemed apparent God had worked behind the scenes to place these precious babies into our arms, but I never imagined the behaviors that would occur as the result of the alcohol exposure.

By the time our girls turned two, we noticed significant developmental delays. As they entered elementary school, problems with short-term memory and judgment became evident. By fifth grade, they experienced learning disabilities, severe anxiety, impaired social skills, various health issues, and numerous hospitalizations. School caused such turmoil that I homeschooled for a couple of years to give my kids individual help and provide flexibility for them to attend physical, occupational, and vision therapies.

My Faith Crisis

I devoted the majority of my time and energy to obtaining the best services to help my daughters develop to their full potential. What I neglected was my relationship with God.

One afternoon, I went into our bedroom walk-in closet and fell to my knees. "Lord," I sobbed, "I know you gave us these children. Then why do I feel as if you've abandoned me? I don't sense your guidance or care. Why would you give us these girls knowing we would suffer so much pain and hardship? How could a loving God do that?"

"Where is the power you're supposed to provide?" I continued on. "If this is what it means to be a Christian, I don't want it."

I cringed, waiting for lightning to come through the roof and strike me dead. I couldn't believe the words that spewed from my lips. Did I really want to walk away from God?

Discovering Joy

One Saturday, I attended a disability conference and listened to a woman speak about her child born with physical disabilities. "When I first saw my daughter, it took my breath away," she said. "There were two small holes where her nose should have been and her eyes were located near her temples." The speaker's final words that day resonated with me: "I believe that God chose this sorrow for our family. And surprisingly, what I at first felt was sorrow, I see now as joy. In all sincerity, if given such a chance, I would not change the journey our family has traveled."

Tears pooled in my eyes as I listened to this mother who had experienced such intense suffering tell of the beauty that resulted from her hardship. I wish I felt the same way, I thought. Is it even possible?

I left that day curious to find out more about joy. While researching the topic, I came upon this quote: "Joy is different than happiness. Biblical joy has nothing to do with physical feelings of pleasure; it has to do with faith and a correct understanding of the character of God. Biblical joy is a posture of unshakeable trust and faith during times of crisis and trial."

Realizing my need for encouragement, I joined a Bible study at a nearby church for moms of kids with disabilities. During the next few years, I learned more and more about God's character, about the power of praise, and about what it means to live with shattered dreams. Gradually, I developed a burning desire to help other moms of kids with disabilities, and I launched a support group at my own church. I started a monthly ministry newsletter and posted twice a week at my disability-related blog. In addition, I became the coordinator for an annual retreat for moms of kids with special needs.

In the meantime, I began freelance writing on topics related to disability and spiritual growth. My work appeared in newspapers, magazines, newsletters, and blogs, and I served a two-year term as a board member for our local Christian writers guild.

My passion for the Bible grew as I spent more time in the Word. I led women's Bible studies and developed and taught classes on how to study the Bible. Currently, I serve as a counselor in our church's Soul Care ministry and am pursuing a certificate in Biblical Studies at a nearby Bible college. As I continue to seek God's face and provide comfort to those who struggle, he gives me peace and contentment in the midst of caring for young adults with mental health issues.

As I look back, I can't say I enjoyed the difficult experiences and pain, but I see how God is working in me to make me more like Jesus. "Consider it pure joy, my brothers, whenever you face trials of many kinds, because you know that the testing of your faith develops perseverance. Perseverance must finish its work so that you may be mature and complete, not lacking anything" (James 1:2–4 NIV 1984).

Joy came as I realized the purpose for my trials and suffering, and as I gained a biblical perspective of the "works of God" in disability (John 9:3). It was a process that started in my closet when God brought me to the end of myself. Like the apostle Paul, I've experienced God's strength in my weakness—the power I had been looking for all along.

Adoption gave me more than children; it gave me hardship that increased the strength and quality of my faith. The storms allowed me to know God more intimately, so that today I'm able to say, "What I at first felt was sorrow, I now see as joy."

Chapter 12

HOW CAN THIS TRIAL HELP ME MINISTER TO OTHERS WHO ARE SUFFERING?

We are commanded to give comfort to people who are suffering. Commanded or not, it is something we will want to do if our faith in Jesus is real. One of the blessings that flows out of a trial is that it will equip us to minister to other people who later go through the same trial. Comfort is not something we store up; we pass it on.

1

Sonny woke up alone in a hospital room and felt for his right knee. It wasn't there.

He knew before the surgery that he would probably lose the leg. The motorcycle accident did a lot of obvious damage. And now what? An athlete and outdoorsman, Sonny knew life was going to be different from now on.

WHY ME? (And Why That's the Wrong Question)

Six months later, in December 1948, Sonny was fitted for his first prosthetic leg. "Bird hunting?" the technician said. "I don't think so, Sonny. That's one of the things you'll just have to give up." Sonny told him to fly a kite. One week later, Sonny was dressing quail, and he's never looked back.

Sonny had a positive outlook in part because he decided to, but it was also because a series of people came into his life and encouraged him to look forward. People like Sister Tarcisius, a bright-eyed nun in the Galveston hospital where Sonny recuperated, who entered the room each day asking, "Do you feel like any fun this morning?" People like a pretty girl down the street who would later become his wife. People like Charlie Gross, who told Sonny that he could still do whatever he wanted in life, which meant something coming from one who suffered childhood polio and spent his life on crutches.

Sonny remembered these people, and all they had meant to him, when a local doctor called years later. The doctor said he had just operated on someone who lost a foot in a motorcycle accident. The patient needed encouragement.

Sonny knew just what to say.

Betty woke up alone in a hospital room and felt for her breast. It wasn't there.

That meant it was cancer. She and her doctor decided before the surgery that if he was pretty sure the lump was malignant, he should take the breast. He was, and he did.

Remember that pretty girl who lived down the street from Sonny? That was Betty. Her mastectomy came more than forty years after Sonny's accident. She felt shock when she realized she had cancer, but not a lot of despair. She really did not know enough about the disease at the time to appreciate its seriousness or to know what she would have to endure. She had not personally known anyone to go through it. How reassuring, then, to receive a visit in the hospital from a breast cancer survivor.

"I brought you a bra!" the visitor said, coming in smiling and bearing the traditional gift from a network of survivors who visit new patients. Now Betty had someone to talk to, who could share what to expect and be a symbol of recovery. The visit meant so much that as soon as she was able, Betty joined the American Cancer Society's Reach to Recovery program so that she could visit, too, and she later coordinated the program for several years. Eighteen years later, Betty estimates that she has visited over four hundred women one-on-one, to do for them what that long-ago first visitor did for her.

That's a lot of bras.

For he gives us comfort in our trials so that we in turn may be able to give the same sort of strong sympathy to others in theirs.
(2 Cor. 1:4 PHILLIPS)

2

What is it that made the polio patient who visited Sonny and the cancer survivor who visited Betty so effective? The question answers itself. They were so effective because they had once been in Sonny's and Betty's place. They faced the same fears and frustrations. They knew what Sonny and Betty were going through and could say, from personal experience, that God would see their new friends through. They were therefore qualified to bring comfort in a way that few other people could. Because people in their own lives had encouraged them, they could pass that encouragement on to Sonny and Betty, and now Sonny and Betty can encourage other people in turn.

That is *exactly* the way it is supposed to work. It's a little like wedding showers. When we get married, friends and family and people we hardly know give us towels and toasters and china we could hardly afford.[1]

WHY ME? (And Why That's the Wrong Question)

Then, we give away butter plates and salad forks for the rest of our lives so that other couples can get the same head start.

Likewise, when we go through a trial, people give us comfort, and then we pass it on once we're on the other side. Paul put it like this, in the form of a praise, which is how it *should* be put:

> All praise to God, the Father of our Lord Jesus Christ. God is our merciful Father and the source of all comfort. He comforts us in all our troubles so that we can comfort others. When they are troubled, we will be able to give them the same comfort God has given us. (2 Cor. 1:3–4 NLT)

He comforts *us* so that we can comfort *others*.

Doing your part?

But he's already made it plain how to live, what to do, what GOD is looking for in men and women. It's quite simple: Do what is fair and just to your neighbor, be compassionate and loyal in your love.
(Micah 6:8a The Message)

3

Giving comfort to hurting people is part of the Christian's job description. Following Jesus is not just about dressing up nice, sitting in a pew, singing the songs, and saying the right words. God saves us to *do* stuff, and religious rituals won't cut it.

> No, this is the kind of fasting I want: Free those who are wrongly imprisoned; lighten the burden of those who work for you. Let the oppressed go free, and remove the chains that bind people. Share your food with the hungry, and give shelter to the homeless. Give clothes to those who need them, and do not hide from relatives who need your help. (Isa. 58:6–7 NLT).

The "religion" God is looking for "is this: to look after orphans and widows in their distress and to keep oneself from being polluted by the world" (James 1:27).

Clearly, we should spend time in prayer and meditate on God's Word. Worship is commanded, too. But if all we do is sit around and think heavenly thoughts, if we never get our hands dirty in the Christian life, then we're doing it wrong.

We are not saved by good works, but we were created to do them (Eph. 2:10). We are to serve "wholeheartedly, as if [we] were serving the Lord, not people" (Eph. 6:7). It's a high standard, because we are supposed to love like Jesus loved (John 15:12), with a self-sacrificial love. A life poured out. And no task is too lowly. After Jesus washed his disciples' stinky feet, he told them it was an example of the kind of service they should perform for each other (John 13:14). After all, acting like a slave is how to become "first" in the kingdom of God (Mark 10:44).

We are to help each other carry burdens (Rom. 15:1; Gal. 6:2). When you see someone hurting, you should feel for them "as if you yourselves were suffering" (Heb. 13:1–3). In the body of Christ, "If one part suffers, every part suffers with it" (1 Cor. 12:26a). Ask what you would need if you were in that person's situation, and then *do* it.

If putting yourself in the other person's place is not motivation enough, then imagine that you are doing it for Christ. Because you are: "I tell you the truth, anything you did for even the least of my people here, you also did for me" (Matt. 25:40 NCV). And if you don't, you're not: "I tell you the truth, anything you refused to do for even the least of my people here, you refused to do for me" (Matt. 25:45 NCV).

When we care for hurting people—when we do good works—it glorifies God (Matt. 5:16). It doesn't have to be a big thing; even a simple cup of water to a child, when that's what is needed, is enough (Matt. 10:42).

It may be simple, but don't kid yourself: loving others by ministering to their needs is a command. And if we know of a good work that we should do and then fail to do it? It's a sin (James 4:17).

Take care of my sheep. (John 21:16)

4

Before we go further with our duty to comfort hurting people, let's eliminate one possible error: it won't save us.

Works (keeping the law) cannot make us righteous. "For it is by grace you have been saved, through faith—and this is not from yourselves, it is the gift of God—not by works, so that no one can boast" (Eph. 2:8–9). The Bible is full of unequivocal statements that we cannot keep the law perfectly, and trying to do so gets us no closer to heaven (Rom. 3:20; Gal. 2:16).

But if it is *faith* that saves us, what kind of faith is required? It's the kind that does something. It's the kind that compels us to love and serve other people. Any other kind of faith is dead.

> Now what use is it, my brothers, for a man to say he "has faith" if his actions do not correspond with it? Could that sort of faith save anyone's soul? If a fellow man or woman has no clothes to wear and nothing to eat, and one of you say, "Good luck to you I hope you'll keep warm and find enough to eat", and yet give them nothing to meet their physical needs, what on earth is the good of that? Yet that is exactly what a bare faith without a corresponding life is like—useless and dead. (James 2:14–16 PHILLIPS)

So good works can't save us. Only faith in Jesus saves us. If that faith is real, though, it can't help but bubble up in the form of love and kindness toward hurting people. Yes, it is commanded, but if we have a real, saving faith, we would *want* to help suffering people whether God commanded us to do so or not.

> *Comfort, comfort my people, says your God. (Isa. 40:1)*

5

At this point, you may be thinking, *but I don't know how to minister to someone in a crisis. I'm not a counselor. I wouldn't have any idea what to say.* That's where your trials come in.

Have you been divorced? Then you know how to minister to people going through a divorce. You know their pain and heartache. You know what they need. You have a qualification for that specific ministry which someone who has *not* been divorced can never have.

Have you lost a child? I met someone at a writer's conference, a fabulous writer, who lost a daughter. He and his wife used their experience to begin a grief support ministry in their church. They can look into a heartbroken parent's eyes and say, yes, they *do* know how it feels. And it will get better.

Been to prison? Go visit people in prison. You know their loneliness and can be a symbol of redemption and hope. Lost a home in a tornado? Volunteer at a shelter after the next one. Gone through a layoff? Help victims of the next round get back on their feet.

Training in counseling would be good for anyone, sure. And there are some situations that require a professional. Still, you have faced some kind of adversity in your life that you can speak to. Be on the constant lookout for people facing the same trial who need encouragement. You're not required to have all the answers, but you can say, "I know where it hurts. I can tell you what came next for me. This is how I dealt with it, here are mistakes I made that you might want to avoid, and this is how I know God loves me."

You get the idea. Your past suffering gives you knowledge and a platform to comfort that you did not have before. That doesn't mean you can only minister to people going through a specific kind of trial, of course.

You can comfort all kinds of people even if you never suffered anything like they have. You have an advantage, though, when the suffering is shared. When it comes to the particular storms you have survived, you have a story to tell and a connection you can draw. When it comes to your own story, you're the expert.

Worried about what to say? Don't be. Follow God in faith, and you can say, "The Sovereign Lord has given me a well-instructed tongue, to know the word that sustains the weary" (Isa. 50:4).

Carry one another's burdens; in this way you will fulfill the law of Christ. (Gal. 6:2 HCSB)

6

Betty and Sonny Booth, featured in the beginning of this chapter, are my in-laws. I love the way their trials did not defeat them and do not define them. One reason this is true, I believe, is that they asked the right questions and looked for ways to use their experiences for good. They both have used their trials as a means to give comfort to others, and the comfort trail doesn't end with them.

Betty, for example, befriended Vicki James. When Vicki heard that she had cancer, she was convinced that it would be her death. But someone visited her, just like someone visited Betty, and helped her hold on to hope. And Vicki later met Betty, who encouraged Vicki to be a part of the breast cancer outreach programs and pass the comfort to others. Vicki is now part of a team that supports and visits other breast cancer survivors. Some of the women Vicki helped have joined support groups and given comfort to yet other survivors. The baton will be passed on again, and again, and again, just like God wants.

If you ever meet Vicki, she will be delighted to share her testimony. That was not always so. Speaking before a group, or about something as serious as cancer, was not something she would have looked forward to before her illness. But that trial, she says, was "the first time I had to deal with something that no one else could fix. I had only God, and I learned that he is enough." As a result, she has an overwhelming desire "to let people know that no matter how dark their hallway is, God can use it for good."

Vicki remembers a sermon about spiritual gifts that she heard before her cancer diagnosis. At the time, she could not see that she had any gifts. Today she will tell you that God has blessed her with the gift of encouragement. Now she is part of a chain of comfort, from one woman, to Betty, to Vicki, to another, and to another, and to another.

Just like it's supposed to work.

> *Therefore encourage one another and build one another up, just as you are doing. (1 Thess. 5:11 ESV)*

7

In one of Jesus' most famous parables, a Samaritan man stopped to give comfort to a crime victim on the side of the road. Jesus' instructions? His takeaway for us from that parable? "Go and do likewise" (Luke 10:37).

Don't look at it as a chore. Sharing comfort is a privilege and a blessing to those who do it. As we "rejoice with those who rejoice, and weep with those who weep" (Rom. 12:15 NASB), we may even find that we get more out of it than the people we serve. Just try to feel sorry for yourself while you're ministering to another person in a trial. I don't think it's possible.

And you won't have to look hard for someone to help. There are hurting people all around us. The trouble for a lot of us is knowing where to start, or having confidence that we won't make things worse. If that's your feeling, then your trials can help. Take time to grieve, ask God the questions on your heart, but then ask this: *How can this trial help me minister to others?*

WHY ME? (And Why That's the Wrong Question)

God gave you comfort when you were the one in trouble. He may have sent other human beings to be his vehicle of encouragement. You know what it meant to you, and now it's your turn. Pass it on to others. Thanks to your trials, you know how.

Now go, and do likewise.

Notes

1. We got five hand mixers as wedding presents. We didn't start out with much, but we could mix just about anything.

Chapter 13

CAN I REALLY REJOICE IN MY TRIALS?

God calls us to rejoice even when we are suffering. The pain itself is not joyful, but when we know God, we can rejoice in his goodness even when our circumstances are awful. We can also rejoice in the good he brings out of our trouble. We cannot have this attitude on our own, but God's Spirit will work in us and teach us to rejoice always.

1

It's hard to get used to a hospital bed in your house. It's even more shocking when it's gone. When it's rolled away, empty.

The bed is gone now, and so is Clay. So are the hospice nurses. The constant flow of people coming by. The ever-increasing pain meds. The worry that if she goes to the grocery, she'll miss the last moment. The waiting.

The clothes, though... they'll stay a while. It's too soon. The familiar scents are too much for Melanie to bear.

There are new things to worry about, too. It will be weeks before the disability benefits start, even though the disability started long ago. A lot of lost income. The girls missing their Daddy. Life without him.

Clay was only thirty-nine, but metastatic melanoma is a monster. It started with a spot the size of a nickel four years ago, and a presence in the lymph nodes, and then surgery, and then apparent remission. Then a spot on the liver, and then his leg. For months nothing changed, but then a scan about six months ago showed that Clay's cancer had gone into overdrive. After forty tumors or so, you might as well stop counting. Radiation and chemotherapy were tried, but they didn't work. Finally, the doctors said they had done all they could. The focus shifted to making Clay as comfortable as possible. And waiting.

Melanie Brewer watched her strong husband fade away. She saw him unable to move for pain, and her unable to help. She took an eight-year-old daughter to the emergency room when the little girl's distress manifested itself in crippling physical pain. And then she buried Clay.

Clay and Melanie's friends grieve with them. Our hearts are broken. We look to the Bible for help and see that God says when we face trials, we should consider it "pure joy" (James 1:2).

Pure joy? Really?

You have *got* to be kidding.

Sorrowful, yet always rejoicing. (2 Cor. 6:10)

2

God has a sense of humor, but I don't think he kids us about his commands or about trials. At first blush, though, it's hard to take seriously a command that we rejoice when everything is falling apart. It's hard to understand how God could require us to feel a certain way, but there is no mistaking that he directs us to "rejoice and be happy in the LORD"

(Ps. 32:11 NCV). He calls us to "sing . . . shout for joy . . . be happy and rejoice with all your heart" (Zeph. 3:14 NCV).

When are we supposed to do this? Apparently, always. "Rejoice always," he says (1 Thess. 5:16). "Rejoice in the Lord always," he tells us again—"and again I say, Rejoice" (Phil. 4:4 KJV).

So . . . always.

We may be tempted to think God is speaking figuratively. He must mean that we should have a joyful attitude in general—that joy is our default position—but that it applies only when things are going smoothly. These rejoicing verses must not apply when unjoyful things happen.

But no. God, who knows how much we love to rationalize, shut that door and specifically says that he wants us to rejoice even when the bullets are flying. And he says it a lot.

James says we should "consider it a great joy, my brothers, whenever you experience various trials" (James 1:2 HCSB). Paul insists that we should "rejoice in our afflictions" (Rom. 5:3 HCSB). And Peter tells us to rejoice "though now for a short time you have had to struggle in various trials" (1 Pet. 1:6 HCSB), and to "rejoice inasmuch as you participate in the sufferings of Christ" (1 Pet. 4:13).

Joy, when you owe more on your house than it's worth? Yes.

Rejoice, when you learn that someone else is getting your spouse's best? Yep.

Joy, when Melanie leaves her dying husband long enough to pick out his gravesite? You bet.

A Christian's joy, you see, does not depend on financial security, or stable relationships, or physical health. It doesn't wax and wane, because it is based on something eternal. God is so good that a believer can have joy even in the middle of her tears. A Christian finds such deep delight in God that there is rejoicing in *spite* of awful circumstances and in the good that results from a trial. It is a joy we experience even when we are sad.

Christian joy is more than a feeling. It is an attitude, a decision to have a love for God that is greater than any knock or bruise or punch that life can throw.

Yes, it's hard to do. Impossible, even, without supernatural help. We can do it, though. If he commanded it, he'll make it possible.

> *I delight greatly in the LORD; my soul rejoices in my God.*
> *(Isa. 61:10a)*

3

One reason we can rejoice in our trials is that no matter what else is going on in our world, we still have God, and he's enough.

One of Peter's quotes in the previous section picked up in the middle of his thought, and we need the rest to understand what he meant. He said, "In all this you greatly rejoice, though now for a little while you may have had to suffer grief in all kinds of trials" (1 Pet. 1:6). Two words are critical to Peter's meaning. The first is "though." The rejoicing comes *although*—in spite of the fact—there is other junk to contend with. Not "because of," but "though."

The second word is "this." We rejoice in "this," which is the cause of our joy. What is "this?" Peter tells us in the preceding verses. No matter what our trials, we can rejoice in God because he has saved us, not only for the future, but also for the present:

> Because Jesus was raised from the dead, we've been given a brand-new life and have everything to live for, including a future in heaven—and the future starts now! God is keeping careful watch over us and the future. The Day is coming when you'll have it all—life healed and whole. (1 Pet. 1:3–5 *The Message*)

"This" is what we rejoice in, "though" we face trials.

And it can never be taken away. Our eternity is secure. Whatever happens *here*, we have a *there* to look forward to, where there will be no more tears and no more death, where we can finally see him face to face and love him unencumbered by sin.

But don't let the thought of there and then make you forget that eternal life is here and now. *Heaven* comes later, but eternal life—life in the Spirit, Christ in us—has already begun (even if we don't always live that way). It's life in the present, Jesus living through you, equipping you to love as he does. It's recognizing your worth and value that come not from your on-again, off-again faithfulness, but from the always-on love of your creator.

Compare that to the things that typically make us happy or sad. Tonight, my favorite college football team lost a game.[1] Big deal, right? Not in the grand scheme of things. But they were contending for a national championship, and that's probably over for this year.[2] It's fun to win, even though I contribute nothing to a victory. It's disappointing to lose, even though I didn't drop a pass, fumble a ball, or jump offside. For some reason, the outcome of games involving players less than half my age, from a college I attended many years ago, affects my mood. (For a while, anyway. I do get over it. Eventually.)

College football is a fun hobby, but what if that was the source of my fulfillment? What if that was where I got my joy? If so, then I would be joyful in good years and have no joy in the off years. A bad call, a penalty, a coaching snafu, or an untimely injury could spoil my whole outlook. It would be silly to depend on something so fleeting and uncertain for all the joy in my life.

And it's just as silly to depend on our career for joy, or a relationship, or financial security, or our health. Not that they shouldn't make us happy. I hope they do. Ideally, our marriages will be a source of great joy, and our jobs will give us much fulfillment, but they shouldn't be the *primary* source of our joy, because they may not last.

God lasts, though. His goodness is something we can count on. His love is eternal, and our salvation is not fleeting. He is holy and perfect, and when we rest in him we see that his goodness outweighs our trials, even the really bad ones.

Job knew this. That's how, with all his problems, he could say, "Though he slay me, I will hope in him" (Job 13:15a ESV). Habakkuk knew this, too. That's how he could rejoice even when everything fell apart. "Though the fig tree does not bud and there are no grapes on the vines, though the olive crop fails and the fields produce no food, though there are no sheep in the pen and no cattle in the stalls, yet I will rejoice in the LORD, I will be joyful in God my Savior" (Hab. 3:17–18).

Can you say this? Is God enough for you? Do you treasure him so much that you delight in him, even in the ICU waiting room? If not, then you're going to have a hard time rejoicing always. Sometimes, maybe, but not always.

Indeed we count them blessed who endure. (James 5:11a NKJV)

4

We can also rejoice in our trials because of the way God uses them in our lives. We've discussed how God can use suffering to draw us near to him, to make us more like his Son, to glorify his name, and to equip us for service. All reasons for joy. In the specific verses about rejoicing during a trial, though, God emphasizes another result of suffering: trials make us buff. Ripped. Toned. Strong and in shape.

We rejoice in trials, James tells us, "knowing that the testing of your faith produces endurance" (1:3 HCSB). Endurance, or perseverance, is the result of a godly approach to suffering. We become more steady. Maybe we break down during the first trial, but as the waves keep coming, we keep our feet more and more. Eventually, we become known as people who keep their cool. We have to stick with it, though. "Endurance must do its complete work, so that you may be mature and complete, lacking nothing" (James 1:4 HCSB). And if we persevere, we are "blessed" and receive the "crown of life" (James 1:12 HCSB).

According to Paul, this endurance yields other benefits. It "produces proven character, and proven character produces hope" (Rom. 5:4 HCSB). "Proven character"—people learn that they can count on you in a crisis. You've been tested. You're reliable. And this reliability produces hope. Hope that we will share in the glory of God's character, that we are being formed more and more into the image of Christ. Hope in a future that can never be taken away. Hope, as in the opposite of despair.

By now, I trust you're convinced that no person is able to avoid suffering completely in this life. Do you want to be the person who keeps her head in a trial or the person who falls apart? If the former, well, that kind of perseverance does not come cheap. It comes from God molding your character through suffering. The ability to keep it together comes through practice, by the grace of God.

And isn't that ability to keep your cool a reason for joy? If the hard times are going to come, it's better to be able to handle them, to *learn* to rely on God. Today's trial prepares you for tomorrow's.

Imagine you knew that in a year's time, you would have to run a half marathon. What would you do over the next twelve months? You would train, obviously. You might start out walking, and then find you could run a mile, and then two. Slowly but surely, you would get into the shape required to finish the race. What you would never do, unless you just wanted to court failure, is wait until the sound of the starter's pistol to take your first step. Paul spoke of the Christian walk in terms of finishing a race (2 Tim. 4:7), and if we want to make it to the end, we need to get in shape. It's suffering that does it.

Like it or not, you haven't been through your last trial. The way you make it through a future trial is determined by whether you let God teach you through the earlier trials. Whether you get buff. Whether you allow God to teach you endurance, character, and hope.

If you understand how valuable these things are, you cannot help but rejoice.

> *You make known to me the path of life;*
> *in your presence there is fullness of joy;*
> *at your right hand are pleasures forevermore. (Ps. 16:11 ESV)*

5

Convinced? Do you believe now that suffering can be a reason to rejoice, or at least that it cannot take away other reasons to rejoice?

Me either, a lot of the time. It's not that I don't believe God or his Word, but the notion of rejoicing during a trial is so opposite of my nature that I want to disregard it. To assume I can't do it. To ignore it, thinking I'll just offer up my I'm-only-human excuses later. For now, I feel a nice pout coming on, and I'll thank you all to leave me be so I can enjoy it.

If that's you, too, I have good news and bad news. The bad news is that our human nature is never an excuse for failing to keep God's commands. The good news is that he is perfectly willing to do in you what you cannot do by yourself.

And you can't rejoice always by yourself. No one ever has, and no one ever will. You cannot simply decide to do it and say, "You know what? I think I'll rejoice today," and then put aside all despairing thoughts. Not by yourself.

When Paul talks about the fruit of the Spirit, he lists joy second, right behind love (Gal. 5:22–23). The fact that joy is a fruit of the Spirit means we can't have it—not the always-on, Christlike joy—without the Spirit working in us. But when the Spirit is within us, the forever-joy is within arm's reach. The Spirit worked in Paul, and he "learned" to be content in all circumstances, whether feast or famine (Phil. 4:11–13).

Joy is a gift, but that doesn't mean we can't turn it down. Just because God is willing to give us a spirit of rejoicing does not mean that we aren't free to decline the gift and be grumpy whenever we want. Which means that while we can't rejoice always by virtue of a simple decision, we do have to decide to accept the work that God wants—that he *longs*—to do in us.

> *Though you have not seen him, you love him; and even though you do not see him now, you believe in him and are filled with an inexpressible and glorious joy. (1 Pet. 1:8)*

Maybe we don't submit right away and allow the Spirit to teach us a joyful attitude. We may need a little distance from our suffering before we can be obedient. Remember in Hebrews, God said that his discipline is unpleasant at the time, but later we can appreciate the work he is doing in our lives (Heb. 12:11). It may be later, down the road, before we are able to look at things God's way. Perhaps it *shouldn't* take us so long to submit, but God is a God of grace and works in our weakness. Marie Hillstrom, whose testimony "My Journey to Joy" appears earlier in this book, describes the process so well. It took time for her to find joy in the hardships that came with adopting daughters with special needs, but she got there. Through prayer, time in the Word, and a humble dependence on God, Marie reached the point where she can say, "What I at first felt was sorrow, I now see as joy."

It can be confusing when the Bible says on one hand that godly joy is solely a fruit of the Spirit, a work of God, and says on the other hand that it is an act of the will and submission on our part. It's hard for me to figure out how it can be both. Remember, though, that rejoicing comes when our love for God is greater than the pain of our trials. Focus on your relationship with him, on seeking always to know him better, and the rest will follow. You'll trip up—we all will—but if we sincerely ask for his help, he will give it.

> *Be glad in the LORD, and rejoice, ye righteous:*
> *and shout for joy, all ye that are upright in heart. (Ps. 32:11 KJV)*

6

Clay and Melanie's situation, with all its sadness, convinces me that we really can rejoice in all circumstances. First is the amazing fact that *they* were able to rejoice. They never doubted God's love, and when their church family ministered to them, they rightly saw it as God blessing them through human hands.[3] I am inspired to hear that Clay's primary prayer was not that God would take away his problems, but that God would give him the strength to make it through whatever God had in store. To hear them say, in spite of what they endured, that God is great and God is good. To see them recognize and appreciate that only God's grace enabled them to make it through their journey. To see that when they were deep in the middle of their own trial, Melanie could still express concern for a friend dealing with breast cancer, instead of thinking only about herself, as I would have done in her place.

When the people who are suffering rejoice, it's much easier for the people around them to do the same (something I hope I will remember when it's my turn). There was potential for us to become bitter, to pull away from God in disappointment that Clay wasn't healed. So many faithful people prayed so hard for a miracle. But when we look closer, we see that their situation was *full* of miracles and full of many reasons to imitate Clay and Melanie's joyful spirit.

We can rejoice in the way God intervened to make Clay's remaining time more meaningful. Just six weeks before Clay died, he and Melanie were able to take a vacation as a couple that was planned long before the cancer reappeared. Few thought Clay would be well enough to go, and he shouldn't have been, but God pulled it off, and they had precious time together. A miracle.

Less than a month before he died, while he was home with hospice care, Clay and Melanie's daughter Christlyn was baptized. Clay was sleeping so much because of his pain medication that no one was sure he would be able to make it to church to see this milestone, or if so, whether he would have enough clarity to be a part of it. He did, and he did. To see the look Clay and Christlyn exchanged was worth a thousand worship services.[4] Another miracle.

We can rejoice in what Clay and Melanie taught us. Watching Clay struggle to stand before the baptism during the praise hymns, holding onto a rail, moving as best he could (he was always one to get down in church), singing along with all his heart that death won't hurt him now, no grave will keep him from his king, "I'm alive, hallelujah!"—well, that's a moment I will never forget. None of us will. How can you sing, "I'm alive," and mean it, when you are on the cusp of death? Clay was just loving God in his own way, when many people wouldn't, and he taught us what the gospel means.

We can rejoice in the strength and energy God gave the family to do what needed to be done. Melanie called it her "crazy strength"—her ability to take care of Clay, of Christlyn and Macy, of other family members going through their own health crises. It came from God and nowhere else, she freely admits.

We can rejoice in the opportunities to minister. God gave the rest of us the chance to show Clay and Melanie God's love through meals, taking the girls out to eat, mowing grass, or whatever other modest things we could do.

We can rejoice in the way God used Clay's sickness to equip his family for service. Melanie speaks of a conviction that God is calling her to some sort of service. She has always been active, but I can't wait to see what God has in store. Grief support? Something related to cancer? I don't know, but I do know that she will be obedient to God's call and is going to have a profound effect in someone's life. And just a few days after the funeral, Christlyn celebrated her birthday by donating her long, beautiful hair to a charity that makes wigs for cancer patients. Now she has short, beautiful hair, and I think she's wise beyond her eight years.

And we can rejoice in the way Clay's death has led people to think about their own salvation. Clay was not the kind of person who would let a little thing like his own funeral stop him from bringing others to Christ. Soon after the service, a couple in our church talked to their daughter about where Clay is now and how that came to be. God obviously had been working in this girl's heart, but God used Clay to take her that last step, and she accepted Christ as her savior.

We have lots of reasons to rejoice in this season of sadness. That does not make it any less sad, but the sadness is coupled with joy. Clay's friends are not masochists, and we aren't rejoicing in the fact that Clay is gone, or for the way Melanie and Macy and Christlyn will miss him, or for the pain he endured, but there are still reasons to rejoice. And knowing where Clay is, that he is cancer-free and whole, that we will one day be with him and again sing, "I'm alive, hallelujah," we can truthfully say that the goodness of God is greater than the awfulness of cancer.

We might be grieving while we do it, but yeah—we're rejoicing.

My comfort in my suffering is this:
Your promise preserves my life. (Ps. 119:50)

7

The hymn writers got it right. Eleanor Hull pleaded that God be her vision, her treasure, "heart of my own heart, *whatever* befall" (italics added).[5]

Horatio G. Spafford wrote that whether he experienced peace or sorrow, "*whatever* my lot," God taught him to say, "it is well with my soul" (italics added).[6] No easy thing to write, as Spafford did, on a ship sailing over the Atlantic where his four daughters perished in a shipwreck.

Can you sing this? Can you call God heart of your own heart, "whatever befall?" Can you say "it is well," whatever your lot?

You can. All who know God can. We can have joy in the face of a job loss, whether we find another one or not, because we know God walks with us and loves us and provides all we really need. We can have joy during illness, however long it lasts, because we know God hurts with us and takes our infirmities upon himself. We can even have joy when death comes around, though it comes too soon, because we know it is not the end.

Each of these trials, and all the others we might have, still hurt. But the joy in God is greater than the pain. It would be crazy to *hope* we lose our job, or get sick, or hear that the doctors have done all they can, just to test these verses out. But if and when the crummy happens, our joy remains. It remains because it is not based on our income or on our physical life, but on the unchanging and perfect goodness of God. And while we are not joyful that a relationship fails or someone we love falls to cancer, we can nonetheless rejoice in what God can do through the trial. Our God fixes broken things, turns water to wine, and brings the dead to life; he can bring good out of any tragedy.

We really can rejoice in our suffering, for no matter what, there is joy in God's presence and "eternal pleasures at [his] right hand" (Ps. 16:11). It's really true that "weeping may stay for the night, but rejoicing comes in the morning" (Ps. 30:5). It's really true that "those who sow with tears will reap with songs of joy" (Ps. 126:5). God really is great, even when our circumstances are not. We *can* sing as we suffer.

We cry, too. Of course we do. Even with all our reasons to sing, sometimes the pain is nearly more than we can stand. But when we cry, we do not cry alone. When we cry, it is with the knowledge that one day all tears will be wiped away. And when we cry, we nonetheless "delight greatly in the Lord; my soul rejoices in my God" (Isa. 61:10a).

Whatever our lot. Whatever befall.

WHY ME? (And Why That's the Wrong Question)

Notes

1. Alabama 24, Texas A&M 29. Doggone those Aggies.
2. Unless Oregon and Kansas State both lose a game. [EDIT: Which they did, the next week. Man are we lucky.] [SECOND EDIT: National champions. Roll tide.]
3. In this video, Clay and Melanie testified about how others loved them when they first began dealing with cancer. The video was made during remission, well before they knew the cancer would return. www.hunterstreet.org/media/ministry/churchwide/glimpses_of_grace/glimpses_of_grace.php?videoName=brewerfamily.
4. Christlyn's baptism video: www.youtube.com/watch?v=68i-X1e8Mq0. You've got to see this.
5. "Be Thou My Vision," Eleanor Hull, 1911.
6. "It Is Well with My Soul," Horatio G. Spafford, 1873.

Mike & Mike (3)

One of the points I have tried to make in this book is that the questions we usually ask—the "why me" questions—are not very helpful. Understandable and normal, but not helpful. But Mike and Mike made that point better than I ever could, because the Reed and Worley families show us that we can choose not to get stuck in navel-gazing mode. We can choose to ask the productive questions of how a trial like cancer can help us grow and how God can be glorified. We can choose to make God's priorities our own priorities, even while we pray fervently for healing and are honest about our fears and frustrations. We can choose to rejoice. We need God's help to make these choices, but it's help he freely gives.

In a trial, as in all of life, we must finish the race. I think from what we have seen so far, there is no doubt Mike and Mike will stay faithful to the end of their trials, however they end.

Reed

Sunday, November 27, 2011, 9:40 PM (April)
I wish I was updating with better news tonight. If you'd asked me yesterday, I would have said I thought Mike was doing better, because he was coughing less and had a good appetite. Unfortunately, today was a different story. He coughed nonstop today, and he ended up at the ER with a nosebleed tonight.... I haven't talked to Mike since he left for the hospital, but I'm positive he is not happy to be admitted. However, they are doing what they feel is best for him. We'd appreciate your prayers, and I'll keep you posted.

Worley

Tuesday, December 13, 2011, 8:39 AM (Pam)

I think back over the last 8 months and remember thinking that when we got (past transplant day,) we would be on easy street. But alas, I am finding that for me, this is the hardest part yet. Every morning for 8 months we woke up, completely dependent on God's grace and mercies to get us through the day. We knew each day was a battle, truly a battle to survive. Then one day, months later, we get our walking papers from the hospital and hugs from the staff and we are done. Finished. We come home and try to find normal life again. Don't misunderstand, I LOVE being home and doing "normal" things again, but something just seems off. I think when you go through any type of trial (and you will go through them!) it would be a shame to go back to exactly the way things were before. To learn nothing from the last 8 months would be sad, almost wasteful I guess. I remind myself during these normal times that God is an everyday god. An hour by hour, minute by minute god. He is not like Hemsi (you know, the ambulance people), who just shows up on the scene when there is an emergency. No, he is always on the scene whether emergency or normal; we just have to seek him, walk with him, feel him.

Reed

Wednesday, December 14, 2011, 8:44 PM (Mike R.)

Good news!! Hey everyone, just wanted to give some much-needed good news. I met with Dr. M yesterday to go over scan results. The verdict is in. . . . Everything as a whole has gotten better. There was a big spot on my liver that was almost reduced by half. There were a few lymph nodes that were totally gone. Long and the short of it, the treatment we are using to treat the MDS is working on the cancer!!

That was much-needed news on our side. There is one new spot on my lung that may be fungal. I don't need problems with my lungs. Please continue to pray for this nagging cough I keep having. It is really wearing me down.

Worley

December 2011 (Pam)

Yes, I'm glad the cancer is behind us, but there are a lot of things I don't want to forget about this year. I don't want to forget that feeling deep in my gut the night Mike told me he had cancer. That reminder that life ends. That there is no guarantee of tomorrow. I don't want to forget driving to CCI for the first time, heart pounding, racing, not knowing what was about to happen. Then immediate peace as friends began praying as we walked through the doors. Perfect peace, no fear. I don't want to forget that incredible feeling when you have a need but haven't talked to anyone but God about it, and then all of a sudden, someone unknowingly fills that need. Miracles, right before my eyes. I don't want to forget that God IS big enough, and that feeling the moment I realized it. I don't want to forget when I first truly understood that His grace IS sufficient and that His power is made perfect in my weakness.

Reed

Wednesday, December 21, 2011, 11:46 PM (April)

As many of you have heard by now, Mike is in ICU in critical condition. As of right now he is stable, but things have been very scary. It all happened super fast. The short story is that he is septic, and he has pneumonia. Please pray. We honestly don't need anything else right now, but I'll let you all know if that changes. He is fighting hard, but he is very sick. As always, thank you.

Thursday, December 22, 2011, 2:26 PM (April)

There hasn't been much change from last night. We talked to Dr. M this morning, and this is what we have feared for years—a serious infection that his body does not have the power to fight off. . . . We know God is in control, and we feel his power.

Thursday, December 22, 2011, 10:45 PM (April)

Mike is healthy and perfect. Heaven welcomed him at 9:30 tonight.

Worley

Tuesday, February 14, 2012, 1:13 PM (Pam)

Cancer free!!! This morning Mike and I met with Dr. McG to get the results from his bone marrow biopsy. The report was: "a full response to treatment, and NO signs of cancer." . . . Funny, although the cancer is gone, I know the journey is not. I still believe this year was not as much about the cancer but about how we would handle everything. So yep, cancer gone, Worley journey continues.

In a way—an important way—both Mikes had a happy ending. Mike Worley is cancer-free, with Pam and his kids now, and I'm thrilled for him. Mike Reed is cancer-free, with his Savior now, and I'm thrilled for him . . . but so sad for April and Trent and the rest of Mike Reed's family.

April and Trent have trials ahead. They will miss their husband and dad terribly. They will grieve, and those who love them will grieve with them. As strong as April was through Mike's sickness, I have no doubt that she takes comfort in the fact that Mike will never hurt again. He will never need another transplant. He will never need another chemotherapy treatment. And I have no doubt that the God who loved them through the chemo will love them through their grief.

Mike Worley is cancer-free at this time, but (sorry Mike and Pam) he won't live forever. None of us will. Mike Worley has not been through his last storm, and he has good times and struggles ahead of him. Whatever happens, though, he and his family are stronger for what they have been through.

I don't know why God allowed a different outcome in these families' lives. However, in both cases, he gave strength and let them feel his love. In both cases, God was glorified by the way these families responded to difficult times.

I only hope that if I ever face a similar situation, I can be half as strong as these families. I only hope that like Mike, April, Mike, and Pam, I am more interested in God's glory than I am in my circumstances.

I only hope that I ask the right questions.

CONCLUSION

He has sent me to bind up the brokenhearted,
To proclaim liberty to captives and freedom to prisoners;
... To comfort all who mourn,
To grant those who mourn in Zion,
Giving them a garland instead of ashes,
The oil of gladness instead of mourning,
The mantle of praise instead of a spirit of fainting.
(Isa. 61:1–3 NASB)

In Alabama, where there may be three snow shovels and one set of tire chains in the entire state, a half-inch of snow will bring a city to a screeching halt. If there is ever a hint of a whisper of a rumor about a snowflake, every grocery and mini-mart will sell out of bread and milk within the hour.[1] I've never understood that. Not once, on the rare occasions when I was snowed in, have I made a sandwich or fixed a glass of milk. I've wished for batteries or a generator, but never for a mug of 2%.

Even if people don't prepare the same way I would, there is something base and fundamental in us all that leads us to prepare for a storm. We can't avoid it, so we might as well be ready. We stock up. Once we're done wrestling for bread we won't eat, we grab some candles and matches, maybe some canned soup. Extra propane for the grill and bottled water. Folks in the path of a hurricane do the same, although they get plywood instead of hand warmers.

> *Yea, the very pleasures of human life men acquired by difficulties.* —St. Augustine[2]

Are you stocked up for your next storm? Not the kind that radar can detect, but the kind that involves a diagnosis, or a layoff, or an I-love-you-but-I'm-not-in-love-with-you conversation? 'Cause it's coming. That or something like it. It may not come today, or even tomorrow. Someday, though, a storm will come.

When it does, there is nothing at the grocery or hardware store that will help you weather it spiritually. Your storm-survival supplies are matters of faith. Beliefs. A dependence on God. The way you make it through your trial will depend a lot on which questions you ask.

Check your pantry. There on the lower shelves, in easy reach, are all the wrong questions—unless you're much stronger and wiser than most, that is. So don't feel bad about them being there. Job and Jeremiah and lots of other people in the Bible asked them, too, and they are probably the first questions you'll reach for when the wind starts howling.

You may ask, "Why me?" But when you do, stop and remember that you won't get an answer. And if we're *all* suffering and *all* asking the same question, does it really make sense to expect to avoid trials and hardship?

You may ask, "Why do bad things happen to good people?" Go ahead. And if you ever meet one of those good people, please let me know. Or if you've figured out how to see through God's eyes into the future so that you can always tell what's best, we would like to hear it.

You might ask if God cares that you're hurting. You wouldn't be the first. If that's your question, though, take time to consider that Jesus left the glory of heaven to enter your world and feel your pain; that he lives

Conclusion

in you now and suffers with you; and that he died so that you could live with him forever. I'd call that caring.

You might ask why God doesn't do something about your suffering, or why he does not simply perform the kind of miracle for you that he did for so many people in the Bible. If that is what's on your mind, take inventory of what God has done for you in the past and what he has promised to do in the future. Keep your eyes open for miracles beyond the one you're most hopeful for. Although it's certainly fine to ask for healing, recognize in advance that God may intervene in another way that is even better than you're capable of imagining.

We all ask the wrong questions at first. We ask in a million different ways why God didn't create a world where no one would hurt or die or cry, but we forget one thing: he did. The world God created started out that way, and one day he will make it so again. Right now, though, we're between Eden and Heaven, and it's going to hurt.

> *There is no pit so deep that God's love is not deeper still.* —Corrie ten Boom

Now that the wrong-question shelf is empty, do you have any other supplies? Are you willing to move past the questions about you and get to some about God?

Will you ask how God can use your trial to draw you nearer to him? He invites you to draw near. He's promised to respond. Your pain can be what he uses to close the gap.

Will you ask how God can use your trial to make you more like Jesus? That is his plan for you. Deep inside, that's what you want for yourself, for your thoughts and actions to be less you-like and more Christlike. Are you willing to search for ways that God can use suffering to discipline you, or prune you, or prove your faith?

Will you ask how God can be glorified in your suffering? He deserves to be glorified, you know. We're pretty much the only part of creation that doesn't do so continuously. When we are hurting, there are unique opportunities for God to be glorified, both through our reaction to the storm and what God can do within it.

Will you ask how your trial can help you minister to others? Every storm is an opportunity to hone our ministry skills. And it is a wonderful way to let other people see God. "No one has ever seen God; but if we love one another, God lives in us and his love is made complete in us" (1 John 4:12).

And finally, will you ask about rejoicing? You might need to ask, because in our fallen nature it isn't intuitive. When you ask this question, though, it turns your focus to God's goodness and provision. It takes you out of yourself, out of your doldrums, and allows you to rejoice even in the middle of your grief. Less grumbling, more praising.

When life is good, enjoy it. But when life is hard, remember: God gives good times and hard times, and no one knows what tomorrow will bring. (Eccles. 7:14 NCV)

There *can* be a song with the tears. There can be peace within the heartache. There can be joy surrounding the pain, if we ask the right questions. Simply asking the right questions can change our attitudes toward suffering and toward God, because when we ask how we can draw near, it means we want to draw near. When we ask how we can be more like Jesus, it means that we want to be more like Jesus. Asking the right questions means we are ready to grow, to mature, to have more faith, to serve, to glorify, to rejoice.

Mike and April Reed found a way. Mike and Pam Worley, Sonny and Betty Booth, Marie Hillstrom, Clay and Melanie Brewer, and others discussed in this book all found ways to ask the right questions. Their trials did not defeat them. They grew and became stronger, closer to God, and more loving to the people around them.

Will you join them? Will you determine now to seek God's help so that you profit from your trial? Will you stock up with faith and sound beliefs? Will you decide now that even if you start out with the wrong questions, you will get past them and on to the right ones?

God will lead you. Through the good times and the bad, whatever your lot, whatever befall, he loves you, he cares for you, and he will lead you to the right questions.

Sometimes 'mid scenes of deepest gloom,
Sometimes where Eden's bowers bloom,
By waters still, o'er troubled sea,
Still 'tis His hand that leadeth me.[3]

Notes

1. I do know of one exception. I spoke to a Birmingham grocer after a rare southern blizzard in 1993. The first two items he sold out of before the storm? Beer and condoms.

2. Saint Augustine, *The Confessions of Saint Augustine: The Eighth Book*, Bartleby.com, www.bartleby.com/7/1/8.html.

3. "He Leadeth Me! O Blessed Thought," Joseph H. Gilmore, 1929.

STUDY QUESTIONS

CHAPTER 1

1. What do you most hope to gain from this study of suffering?

2. When have you asked, "Why me?" Did you ever find an answer?

3. What are your greatest fears? If they come to pass, what will they do to your faith?

4. There is no question that there is suffering in the world. Is the existence of suffering consistent with your views of God? Why or why not?

5. When it comes to the question of *why* there is suffering in the world, what do you find satisfying, or unsatisfying, in the answers proposed by (a) C. S. Lewis? (b) Rabbi Harold Kushner? (c) God, in his answers to Job in chapters 38–41?

6. God chose not to explain to Job all the reasons Job had suffered such tragedy. Why might God withhold that information?

7. How were Job's friends helpful? How were they unhelpful?

8. You may have heard of "the patience of Job." Do you think Job was patient?

9. Read Psalm 22.
   a. Does David feel like God has abandoned him? What indicates that he does, or does not, feel this way?

   b. Does David trust God?

   c. How can David write both verse 1 and verse 22?

CHAPTER 2

1. What qualities of human nature cause us to believe that suffering does not just hurt but that it is somehow *unfair*?

2. What qualities of human nature make us want to help victims of a natural disaster?

3. Is there any overlap in the lists you made responding to the first two questions? What does that tell you about our beliefs concerning suffering?

4. How has a trial made you feel helpless, or like you are not in control of your circumstances?

5. Does your attitude toward pain and suffering differ when it appears that you brought the problem on yourself through bad decisions, versus when you suffer through no apparent fault of your own? Why or why not?

6. What recent natural disasters have seemed especially tragic to you?

   a. What seemed most tragic to you about these disasters: The *amount* of suffering? The apparent *randomness* of the destruction? A personal connection to a victim? Something else?

Study Questions

    b.   Why did that aspect of the disaster bother you the most?

    c.   How did communities come together after those disasters to help people in need?

7.   Read Isaiah 40:27–31.
    a.   Does this passage suggest that it is wrong to feel "disregarded" by God?

    b.   When we feel that way, what does God wish us to know?

    c.   What does it mean to "hope in the Lord" in the face of disaster?

CHAPTER 3

1.   Put this comment from the Book of Job into your own words: "Man is born to trouble as surely as sparks fly upward" (Job 5:7).

2.   How did Jesus suffer in ordinary and human ways?

3.   How did Jesus suffer in unique or extraordinary ways?

4.   What was Jesus' attitude toward his suffering? Can you think of any times when, like most of us, he would have preferred *not* to suffer?

5.   What do you think it means that God has set eternity in our hearts? (Eccles. 3:11). What does that have to do with our attitude toward suffering?

6.   Where does the idea come from that if we are "good enough" we should be able to escape pain?

7. In what ways are the storms we go through temporary?

8. As much as you may be looking forward to heaven, how does the hope of heaven help *now*?

9. There has been, and will continue to be, a lot of talk about pain and trials in this book. Let us never forget that God gives us great gifts and that there is much in this life to be grateful for. List five blessings for which you can give thanks to God.

10. Read Ecclesiastes 1:1–9; 2:17–18; 7:2–3; 9:1–6; and 12:13–14.
    a. According to Solomon, how likely is it that a person will know pain?

    b. Why does Solomon find work and pleasure to be meaningless?

    c. Why is it better to "go to a house of mourning than a house of feasting?"

    d. With this bleak view of man's fate, how does Solomon find meaning in life?

CHAPTER 4

1. Whose suffering seems the most tragic or unfair to you? Is your view based on your relationship to the person, your opinions about the person's moral character, or some other factor?

2. If we believe that a particular trial is "unfair" because the person suffering has good moral character, does that mean (a) that *someone else* should be suffering the trial instead, or (b) that *no one* should be living through that trial?

a. If someone else, how do we choose who that person should be?

   b. If no one, how realistic is our expectation?

3. Why is it comforting to believe that another person's sins are worse than our own? How is this view consistent or inconsistent with God's view?

4. Why do we sometimes assume that a person who is suffering must have committed a sin and called the suffering on himself? What does Jesus say about such assumptions?

5. Should we ask God to give us what we deserve? Why or why not?

6. Put the following statement by Jesus into your own words: "And why worry about a speck in your friend's eye when you have a log in your own? How can you think of saying to your friend, 'Let me help you get rid of that speck in your eye,' when you can't see past the log in your own eye?" (Matt. 7:3–4 NLT).

7. Read Psalm 51. What is the source of David's suffering? What is his prayer? What questions do you think David asked about his suffering (and what questions *didn't* he ask)?

CHAPTER 5

1. What prevents us from knowing what is best for our lives?

2. How were the trials of Joseph and Esther a blessing to them? To others?

3. What about Jesus' crucifixion was a terrible trial to endure? Why might Jesus nonetheless say that it is a good thing that the crucifixion occurred? Why might we?

4. How might enduring the following trials be of benefit to someone?
    a. A job loss?

    b. A nonfatal illness?

    c. A house fire where no one was injured?

5. If we witness someone suffering through such trials and believe that they will be better off in the long run, should we still sympathize with them and minister to them while they are in the middle of it? Why or why not?

6. What trial have you been through that seemed terrible at the time, but in the end was a benefit to you? What was it about the trial that was a benefit?

7. Why might God choose to give us step-by-step direction instead of revealing his entire plan to us at once?

8. Read Psalm 142.
    a. What words does David use to describe his trial? To describe God?

    b. Do you see any benefit that may come to David for enduring his trial?

    c. Does David's comment in Psalm 119:67 bring a possible benefit to mind?

CHAPTER 6

1. What evil or suffering have you seen that made you wonder if God cared about the victims (else he would have stopped it)?

2. What evidence do we have that God takes no pleasure in our suffering?

3. Why would Jesus touch a leper (Mark 1:41), sigh when healing a deaf and mute man (Mark 7:34), and cry at Lazarus's funeral?

4. What does it matter that Jesus suffered as a man in the same way that we suffer?

5. What do you think Dr. Paul Brand meant when he said that God "is in you, the one hurting, not in it, the thing that hurts?"

6. If God takes no pleasure in our suffering, why do you think he does not simply end all suffering and eradicate all evil from the world?

7. The disciples knew Jesus cared about their peril when he miraculously stopped the storm. How can we be sure of God's love if he chooses *not* to remove our trial?

8. Read Psalm 77.
    a. What did the psalmist do when he felt like God did not care about him?

    b. Why would this help?

    c. What is it specifically that you can remember about God to encourage you when God seems distant?

WHY ME? (And Why That's the Wrong Question)

CHAPTER 7

1. Think back on trials and natural disasters you listed in response to questions in earlier chapters. Although God allowed those trials to happen and did not remove all ill effects, how was he at work?

2. Why did Cleopas and other followers of Jesus feel defeated after Jesus died on the cross? What was it that they misunderstood about the crucifixion?

3. Because of the cross, we can be with God for all eternity in heaven. But how does the cross help us *now*?

4. How would you describe the work of the Holy Spirit in a believer's life?

5. Assume someone commits a violent crime and is never caught by law enforcement. How can we be sure that justice will be done? What forms might it take?

6. How, and when, is justice done to the "wicked and ruthless man" in Psalm 37:35–36?

7. How was God at work when Habakkuk wondered why God allowed so much injustice in Israel? What about God's plan was disturbing to Habakkuk?

8. Read Lamentations 3:19–33, where Jeremiah mourns Israel's exile in Babylon.
   a. Was God "doing something" when his chosen people were in exile?
   b. How did Jeremiah praise God even when he grieved? For what characteristics of God?

CHAPTER 8

1. When has God not answered your prayers in the way that you hoped?

2. Why might you feel cheated if God does not heal you or the one you love?

3. If we think of Jesus' miracles as sermons, what message was he giving us through his wonders?

4. Imagine that you lose your sight and pray for a miracle. Other than restoring your vision, what other miracles might God perform in your life?

5. Why is God more qualified than we are to identify our greatest needs? To decide what miracle will be best for us?

6. Read Mark 14:35–36.
    a. What did Jesus pray for before the crucifixion?

    b. How did Jesus qualify his request?

    c. How did God answer Jesus' prayer?

    d. Does it surprise you that God did not say yes to every prayer Jesus uttered? Why or why not?

7. What does it mean to "submit to God and be at peace with him?" (Job 22:21).

8. Read Psalm 34.

a. Do verses 8–10 mean that a Christian will never be poor, or that no Christian has starved to death? What *is* the meaning of this passage?

b. What kind of deliverance and protection does David refer to in verses 19 and 20?

CHAPTER 9

1. What does it mean to be "near" to God?

    a. What must God do for us to be near to him?

    b. What is our part in the equation? What must *we* do in order to be near to God?

    c. How do Christian disciplines such as prayer and Bible study help us to have intimacy with God?

2. Think of the married couples you know who have seemed especially close to each other. What did they have in common? How much of their intimacy was accidental, and how much of it was the result of a willingness to work on the relationship?

3. Now think of the people who seem to be especially on fire for Christ. What do they have in common? What do these people *do* that helps them be and feel near to God?

4. When have you felt near to God? Was it a time of prosperity or a time of need? When you felt distant from God, was it a time of prosperity or need?

5. If you were Hosea, could you take Gomer back? How does Hosea's story make you view God's love?

6. If you were Gomer, would you accept Hosea's offer of reconciliation?

7. Do you truly believe that God wants you to be near him even when you treat him the way Gomer treated Hosea?

8. Read Psalm 78.
    a. How could the people forget God's past providence (verse 11)?

    b. When were the Israelites near to God, and when did they stray (verses 32–38)?

    c. What did God use other than pain in an effort to reach his people?

    d. Why do you think pain is what finally caused them to draw near to God?

CHAPTER 10

1. Why do you discipline your children? Or, why did your parents discipline you?

2. How have you changed since you became a Christian? What sinful behaviors or attitudes used to be a struggle but no longer control you?

3. Has God encouraged you to trim any part of your life that may not have been sinful but that took time or energy away from service? How so?

4. Did God use suffering to make any of the changes listed in your response to the previous two questions? What trials were they, and how did they lead you to change?

5. Read 1 Samuel 17:32–37.
    a. How had David's faith been tested in the past?

    b. How did the earlier testing help as David prepared to confront Goliath?

    c. What can you do to help you remember the ways God has provided for you in the past?

6. Moses lived in Pharaoh's palace for the first forty years of his life, but God sent him to tend sheep for another forty years before calling him from the burning bush. What might Moses have learned in the desert that he was less likely to learn in the palace?

7. What are your reactions when you meditate on the sufferings of Christ? Do those thoughts impact your behavior? How?

8. Read Psalm 39.
    a. How would you describe David's view of life? Of mankind?

    b. Why might David ask God for help in understanding how fleeting life can be?

    c. Where is David's hope? Why there?

CHAPTER 11

1. God is perfectly magnificent whether we acknowledge it or not. Why does he command us to praise him?

Study Questions

2. Why does God deserve our praise?

3. God shows his glory through his creation and in many other ways, and one of those is through his church. You and me. What grade would you give the Christian church today for reflecting the Lord's "shining greatness?"

4. How has God been glorified through your trials?

5. If a person faces a terminal illness, what are different ways God might choose to intervene? How could each of these possible miracles reveal God's glory?

6. Now think of the different ways that this person with a terminal illness could respond to his bad news. Describe a response that would glorify God, and contrast it with a response that may not.

7. Paul says you should not grieve as one who has "no hope." Hope in what?

8. When you share what God has done in your life, what benefit does that give the listener? The speaker?

9. Read Psalm 145.
    a. What mighty acts of God are told from generation to generation?

    b. What trial or suffering gave God the opportunity to do these works?

    c. In fact, can you think of a wondrous work of God that did not arise out of some sort of trial or suffering?

    d. What has God done in your life that you can share with others?

e. Who, specifically, can you tell?

CHAPTER 12

1. Why is God more interested in "mercy" than "sacrifice" (i.e., religious ritual)? (Hosea 6:6). How do many people get this backwards?

2. Why does God consider our ministry for others to be ministry to *him*? (Matt. 25:31–46).

3. Imagine that a friend loses his or her spouse, and you have never gone through that particular loss.
    a. If you try to comfort that friend, what barriers would you face that a widow or widower would not?
    b. What kind of things could a widow say to your friend that you could not?
    c. Even if you have not been through the same trial, what comfort can you offer?

4. What trials have you gone through that could open doors to ministry?
    a. What specifically did you learn that would be a comfort to someone going through the same trial?
    b. Who gave you comfort when you were suffering? What did people say that made you feel better? What things did well-meaning people say that did *not* make you feel better?

5. Why might a person who has been through a trial *want* to give comfort to others?

6. How does ministering to other people bless the person doing the ministry?

7. Read Psalm 10:12–15 and Psalm 146:7–9.
   a. What is God's attitude toward hurting, grieving, and helpless people?

   b. What are the promises of God that such people can rely upon?

   c. How can God use ordinary people—you and me—to keep those promises?

CHAPTER 13

1. Is there a difference between joy and happiness? How would you distinguish these terms?

2. What do you have to be thankful for even if everything else is lost?

   a. What characteristics of God are worth rejoicing in?

   b. What has God done for you, or what has he promised, that is worthy of rejoicing?

3. What earthly things give you joy? Could you still rejoice if you lost them?

4. How do you know that God loves you?

5. How levelheaded were you during your last trial? Has your endurance increased over the course of your life, or are trials becoming harder and harder to handle?

6. Looking back at that most recent trial, did you rejoice in God at the time? Or, did there come a point, after God worked in your heart, when you were able to rejoice?

7. When do you find it most difficult to have a joyful attitude?

8. Why are joyful people more fun to be around? Do you think non-Christians would be more willing to listen to what you have to say about God if they thought of you as a joyful person?

9. What can you do to become more joyful?

10. Read Psalm 66.
    a. Why does the writer say he rejoices? (List several reasons given in the psalm.)
    b. Which of these reasons are causes for you to rejoice as well?
    c. What phrases show that while the writer rejoices, he has also known suffering?
    d. Does the writer's joy depend on his circumstances? Why or why not?

CONCLUSION

1. Has this study changed your view of suffering? How?

2. Has this study changed your view of God and his love? How?

3. Who discussed in this book responded to trials in a way you hope to imitate if you ever face something similar? What about their response is admirable to you?

Study Questions

4. What thought or statement in this book do you most disagree with? Why? What Scripture would you like to bring to the author's attention to straighten him out?

5. Why might you not want to discuss some of these teachings with someone who is in the middle of an intense trial? How might you minister to him or her instead?

6. How does our perception of God change when someone we know dies of cancer (like Clay Brewer or Mike Reed), versus when someone we know survives cancer (like Mike Worley or Betty Booth)? Has God changed, or is our perception off?

7. Many people who shared their stories for this book said something like this when I interviewed them: "I know it sounds crazy, but now that I'm through this trial, I wouldn't trade it for anything." Why might someone say that? Do you think it's crazy?

8. Why do you agree or disagree with the following quotes from Corrie ten Boom and Saint Augustine, respectively?

    a. "There is no pit so deep that God's love is not deeper still."

    b. "Yea, the very pleasures of human life men acquired by difficulties."

9. Read Psalm 63. Could you say this, and mean it, during a trial?

10. On a scale of one to ten, how ready are you for your next trial? What can you do to bump that number up?

BIBLIOGRAPHY

Books
Boyd, Gregory. *Is God to Blame?* Downers Grove, IL: InterVarsity, 2003.
Kushner, Harold S. *When Bad Things Happen to Good People*. New York: Random House, 2001.
Leibniz, Gottfried. *Essays on the Goodness of God, the Freedom of Man and the Origin of Evil*. Translated by E. M. Huggard. Peru, IL: Open Court, 1985.
Lewis, C. S. *The Problem of Pain*. New York: HarperCollins, 1940.
MacArthur, John. *Twelve Ordinary Men*. Nashville: Thomas Nelson, 2002.
Walsh, Sheila. *Life Is Tough But God Is Faithful*. Nashville: Thomas Nelson, 1999.
Wilkinson, Bruce. *Secrets of the Vine*. Colorado Springs: Multnomah, 2001.
Yancey, Philip. *Disappointment with God: Three Questions No One Asks Aloud*. Grand Rapids: Zondervan, 1992.

Articles
Barry, Dan. "Losing Everything, Except What Really Matters." *New York Times*, April 30, 2011. www.nytimes.com/2011/05/01/us/01land.html?pagewanted=all.
Barry, Ellen. "A Child in Charge of '6 Babies.'" *Los Angeles Times*, September 6, 2005. www.chicagotribune.com/news/nationworld/chi-0509060168sep06,0,3659601.story.
Cross, Kim. "What Stands in a Storm, Part III: Fellowship." *Southern Living Magazine*, August 2011. www.southernliving.com/general/tornado-stories-what-stands-in-a-storm-fellowship-00417000074347.
Gould, Izzy. "Tuscaloosa Pastor Encourages Flock at Outdoor Sunday Service, the First after Tornado." *Huntsville Times*, May 1, 2011. http://blog.al.com/live/2011/05/tuscaloosa_pastor_encourages_f.html?mobRedir=false.

Hicks, Tommy. "Carson Tinker Belongs among Heroes—And Not Just the Sports Kind." *Mobile Press-Register*, December 9, 2011. www.al.com/sports/index.ssf/2011/12/carson_tinker_belongs_among_he.html.

Hix, Lisa. "Katrina as a Blessing: It Sent One Teen Here." SFGate.com, August 27, 2006. http://articles.sfgate.com/2006-08-27/opinion/17308554_1_bus-hurricane-katrina-neighbors.

Editorial Board. "We Are Neighbors, All of Us." *Huntsville Times*, May 1, 2011. http://blog.al.com/breaking/2011/05/madison_county_tornadoes_we_ar.html?mobRedir=false.

Websites

Hunter Street Baptist Church. Brewer Family Testimonial. Video. www.hunter-street.org/media/ministry/churchwide/glimpses_of_grace/glimpses_of_grace.php?videoName=brewerfamily.

Toomer's for Tuscaloosa. http://ToomersforTuscaloosa.com. www.facebook.com/toomersfortuscaloosa.

Ministry of Alistair Begg. www.truthforlife.org

CIA World Factbook. Washington, DC: Central Intelligence Agency, 1997. UM-St. Louis Libraries Edition, derived and modified by Raleigh Muns April 20, 1998. www.umsl.edu/services/govdocs/wofact97/country-frame.html.

Christlyn Brewer's Baptism. Video. October 14, 2012. www.youtube.com/watch?v=68i-X1e8Mq0.

Thomas Cole, *The Voyage of Life*, National Gallery of Art.
Childhood—www.nga.gov/fcgi-bin/timage_f?object=52450&image=12547&c.
Youth—www.nga.gov/fcgi-bin/timage_f?object=52451&image=12552&c.
Manhood—www.nga.gov/fcgi-bin/timage_f?object=52452&image=12558&c.
Old Age—www.nga.gov/fcgi-bin/timage_f?object=52453&image=12564&c.

Hymns

Anonymous. "Just a Closer Walk with Thee."
Hull, Eleanor. "Be Thou My Vision." 1911.
Gilmore, Joseph H. "He Leadeth Me! O Blessed Thought." 1929.
McAfee, Cleland B. "Near to the Heart of God." 1903.
Robinson, Robert. "Come, Thou Fount of Every Blessing." 1757.
Spafford, Horatio G. "It Is Well with My Soul." 1873.